CONGRESS SURE CAN RUIN A GOOD PARTY!!!

A seriously lighthearted look at the White House, our Government and Society in general

By Marilyn Ward

Page Intentionally Left Blank

Congress Sure Can Ruin a Good Party

Political Humor with a Touch of Sobering Reality

Marilyn L. Ward

Page Intentionally Left Blank

ISBN-13: 978-1975868932

ISBN-10: 1975868935

First CreateSpace Printing: August 27th, 2017

Page Intentionally Left Blank

INTRODUCTION

Let me begin by telling you a little about myself and my purpose for writing this book. My name is Marilyn Ward. I am a twice divorced proud mother of three and just as proud grandmother of two beautiful granddaughters and one awesome grandson. I probably have no business writing as I have no writing experience, but I am truly frustrated and frankly mad at the congressional gridlock in Washington. I have always loved writing and have spent a lot of time on Facebook which has been well received for the most part. Some of course do not appreciate my political opinions being expressed on Facebook, so I decided to try a slightly different format.

As my friends and family will attest, I have a rather quirky sense of humor. I am originally from the Midwest after all. Wisconsin to be exact. I have perfected my sarcasm and humor over my 68 years. Now that I think about it, perfected may be just a tad strong, but I'm going with it anyway. Sometimes my humor doesn't translate well into writing. You need to "hear" me. So, this could be a real challenge for me. I moved to Arizona in 1987, but my humor tagged along. I'm sure a few people wish I'd left it there. Hey! You just can't please everybody.

I try very hard to be fair to both sides of the aisle. I have registered as both Republican and Democrat over the years. I used to consider myself a true

Independent. Since the Republican Party allowed the Tea Party to play along; I must say I am now true blue. Sorry Republicans, but I think you blew it there!

While I am a wary Democrat, I try to be fair when I see any injustice being done. It doesn't matter if it's done by the Republicans or the Democrats. I will call them out! I believe I speak for most of middle or lower-class Americans who do not speak out enough. We all talk **to** each other, but rarely do we use our voices when it comes to the polls or call our Congress. We do not believe our voices matter. That's why I'm writing this book. I hope it speaks to you in an entertaining fashion. I hope it stimulates your thinking. It is more political commentary than anything, sprinkled with facts and hopefully things to make you laugh. It is not meant to offend anyone of any political affiliation. It is simply my take on Washington, the current administration, society in general and what steps might be taken to fix things. I hope you enjoy the book.

Please keep in mind however, this book in strictly my opinion. I have done my very best to fact check, but in no way, should this be used as any type of reference material. That would make you even nuttier than me. Not to mention you wouldn't be happy with the grade you'd get should you use it as a reference for a college thesis. You're just going to have to take my word for it, ok? Now as they used to say, "On with the show!".

Page Intentionally Left Blank

DEDICATION

This is a difficult, if not impossible, dedication to make as there are just so darned many people that I would like to dedicate this book to. Of course, there are the obvious suspects, my children, my grandchildren, my parents, my family and friends of whom there are so many that are so deserving; to pick only one person was a nearly impossible task. Of course, my first thought was of my mom. After much soul searching however, I finally decided that perhaps the best route to go was to dedicate this book to someone who is still living.

I love and miss my mom every day of my life, but she is no longer here to enjoy it. At last, I finally decided on the one person who I feel has shaped my childhood and some of my earliest memories in a positive and consistent way. He was always there to support me, no matter how stupid my mistakes may have been. So, this was my choice. I am sure I made the right one, although it was difficult. We do not always agree on certain political issues or even religious ones, but there is nothing I wouldn't do for him and he knows that. I have the deepest respect for his beliefs, even when they may not be in alignment with my own.

I am dedicating my first book to my Uncle Floyd. My earliest memories as a child are of my dad and my uncle taking me to the park on Sundays. My Uncle Floyd would push me on the swings "higher than the sky". I was 7 years old when he married my Aunt Pat. I was absolutely thrilled to be their little flower girl. When my Aunt and Uncle call me Mo, it still makes my heart melt just a little. Hearing that familiar childhood nickname is just so special when it comes from the people you love most in this world.

So, Uncle, this book is dedicated to you. I hope I've made you proud. I simply adore you.

Page Intentionally Left Blank

TABLE OF CONTENTS

CHAPTER 1

Tag! You're it!

How many of you remember playing tag as a kid? I used to love that game. I was lousy at it, but I loved it. My sharp turns were atrocious, so I always got caught and I had a terrible time catching the other kids too. Most kids these days probably aren't even familiar with the game as it isn't played on a computer or TV screen. Too bad, but that's not what I'm referring to in this scenario.

Aside from the game, I really don't like it when we apply "tags" to certain groups. I'm odd that way. Of course, I'm sure I've been just as guilty as anyone else from time to time, but for the most part I really do try to stay away from them.

The tags that I have been hearing a lot of lately refer to the Democrats and the Republicans. I don't understand why it is that we seem to feel that all Democrat are elitists or rich and smart. Is that to assume that if you are a Republican, you are dumb and poor? These tags are ridiculous. While I am more of a moderate than anything, my beliefs lie more along the Democratic lines. I believe in women's rights, gay rights, religious freedom, all kinds of rights. I also believe in gun legislation.

No, I'm not saying we need to take everyone's guns away, but I sure would like to see a ban on assault weapons. I once had someone tell me they liked them because they were "fun to shoot". Ok, fine. Then why not shoot them off at a gun range? If it's that much fun, you shouldn't mind paying to rent one. There you go. That's my story and I'm stickin' to it.

Back to the "tags". While I am a Democrat in my beliefs, I am anything but rich or elite. I fall at the bottom of the food chain people. While I think cutting taxes sounds great in theory, we simply can't both cut taxes and still offer greater infrastructure, airports, healthcare, law enforcement, etc., etc. It simply makes no sense.

Where do you think that money is going to come from? Has anyone been paying attention to how much our current President is costing this country just in his weekend travels and protection for his wife and son while living in New York? The cost is enormous. His security detail alone has outspent any other President that I am aware of in such a short amount of time.

Our President and the rest of the Republican party for some strange reason is adamantly opposed to taxing the rich at a higher tax rate. Why? I think I may have some idea, but I'm a little out there, so you can just take this for what it's worth. I think they're the ones who actually have most of the money. Did you really think that Trump was going to go into office and tax the heck out of his own company and himself as well as his friends/loyalists? I sure didn't.

From the one-page tax reform bill he submitted it turns out he did quite the opposite. He gave the biggest tax breaks to the rich and the upper middle class, leaving the rest of us to somehow pick up the slack. It's called the "trickle-down effect". Does it work? Well, I haven't seen it work yet. It's been somewhat of a temporary fix in the past at its' best; but never long-term. Don't get me wrong. I'm not suggesting we leave the entire tax burden to the rich.

They've earned their money and they shouldn't be expected to support those of us who don't have as much just because they have more than we do. Not at all.

What I do object to, however, is some of the legal loopholes that the rich can take advantage of to avoid paying their "fair share". Why should a father of 3 earning $60,000 pay a higher percentage of taxes than a millionaire just because he can't take advantage of certain write-offs? That's a problem that Washington could resolve and it's a promise that Trump made during his campaign. I didn't see that in his tax reform proposal, but then we still haven't seen the finished product.

Hopefully, it will be more comprehensive and it will address some of these issues. That's one campaign promise I really hope he keeps.

My point is this, I take offense to it when I hear people call me a "liberal" or an "elitist" just because I happen to believe in most things Democrat. I am far from rich and I am not even totally liberal as I consider myself to be more moderate. Yes, I can be opinionated sometimes and I am strong willed for sure, but I am not an extremist. When I try to look at any given political situation, I try to look at it through the "other side's" point of view to see how they would look at it. Sometimes, it helps me form a slightly different opinion. There are many times when I do not like what the Democrats do. Yes, my values and beliefs are in line with theirs, but I do not always agree with their methods. I'm usually mad at them just as often as I am at the Republicans these days. Washington simply isn't working right now and both sides are to blame, not just one.

Not all Democrats are elite, smart and rich and not all Republicans dumb and poor, so what if we dump the tags and go back to playing tag in the front yard like we did when we were kids? It's far more fun.

This Page Intentionally Left Blank

CHAPTER 2

THE RUSSIANS ARE COMING! THE RUSSIANS ARE COMING!

As I am writing this book, Sally Yates and Jim Clapper are being questioned by Congress regarding the Michael Flynn investigation as well as Sally Yate's refusal to follow the President's direction when she refused to approve the first "travel ban". I must admit my head is literally spinning. Yes, I can do that! I'm a whole lot of fun at parties, depending on the crowd. I can either be the life of the party or I can help the host clear her guests out early if needed. Like I said; it just depends on the crowd. Let me get on with the book before I go too crazy.

I do not recall a time in all of history where so many government officials have been tied to Russia. Here's a list of all the "President's Men" that to date have been accused of having dealings with Russia. Pay attention now, you don't want to miss this.

(1) Roger Stone — Former Trump Advisor
(2) Rex Tillerson — Secretary of State
(3) Paul Manafort — Fmr Trump Campaign Mgr
(4) Michael Flynn — Fmr National Security Advsr
(5) Jeff Sessions - Attorney General
(6) Carter Page — Foreign Policy Advisor
(7) Steve Bannon — Chief Strategist
(8) Jared Kushner — Trump Advisor
(9) J.D. Gordon — Trump Security Advisor

There are nine so far. No, really! This is no joke. Now I get it to some degree, as we are dealing with people that are coming from a world of business and not the political realm. I might not be as surprised by this if it were just people like Rex Tillerson or even Jeff Sessions, but the rest I have some serious problems with. There are simply too darned many of them for one thing.

I believe that Tillerson's dealings with Russia prior to his appointment were purely on a business level and what he has done since has nothing to do with the other. I'm not quite as confident about Sessions, but it's based more on my gut than what he's said or anything else frankly. I have through bad experiences learned when people are not to be believed.

Both Sessions and especially Carter Page (or as I like to call him, "Cagey") do not sound the least bit believable. I could of course, be wrong.

It's been known to happen a time or two.

As for Mike Flynn, not to toot my own horn or anything; but I had that guy pegged from the very beginning as someone to keep a close eye on. I just knew he was up to no-good and these hearings are certainly starting to prove that my gut was right. My mom used an expression "crooked as a dog's hind leg". Perhaps some of you are familiar with it. I think it fits Flynn perfectly. Between him and "Cagey"; I'd be shocked if they didn't end up in jail for some sort of crime.

I find it hard to believe that all these people had ties to Russia on various levels without our President having any knowledge of such activity. If he didn't, perhaps he should keep his thumbs down more often and try keeping his fingers on the pulse of the people surrounding him. He needs to become more involved with what's happening in his own White House rather than on Twitter, Late Night talk shows or Cable News. He's like a 14-year-old boy who just got his first I-Phone and can't stop himself.

Why can't someone take his toys away when he starts to bully or behave badly? I just don't get it. Isn't there a grown-up in the house that can keep an eye on him? Is that really asking too much?

OK, HOLD THE PHONE! BREAKING NEWS!! James Comey was just fired from the FBI. Do my ears deceive me? The President just fired Comey because the Deputy Attorney General Rod Rosenstein advised the President that Comey had grossly exaggerated both the number and the relevance of the emails that were released a mere eleven days prior to the election. Huh! Does that sound right to you guys? Something sounds a little off here.

While I would agree that if, in fact, Comey truly gave classified testimony indicating that perhaps the prior information he had given was deceiving; he should be punished, what I am not buying is the fact that President Trump would give a dog's behind about that. He has done nothing but praise Comey in fact, for releasing those emails. To make matters even more interesting, Comey is right in the middle of investigating Trump and his band of merry men regarding Russia.

Both Democrats and Republicans are questioning the timing of Comey's firing. As if things weren't bad enough, the poor guy wasn't even told face to face. He was actually giving a speech in L.A. when he saw it on television. At first, he thought it was a prank. He called his office and one of his aides opened the letter from Trump stating he had been fired. Really? How tacky is that?

Our President was polite however. He even made it a point to thank Mr. Comey for assuring President Trump on three separate occasions that "he" was no longer being investigated. I smell a rat. Something tells me "The Donald" would not be a very good card player.

Since this story first broke, we have learned that in fact, the President had invited both Mr. Rosenstein as well as Jeff Sessions to the White House the day before. Supposedly, he asked

Rosenstein to write the letter advising that it would be in the best interest of the country to let Comey go. Jeff Sessions had recused himself from any investigations involving either Russia or Hillary Clinton. So why was he there?

How do we even know that this is true? Beats me! I don't think we can get the truth out of Washington at all anymore. I honestly don't trust either side. That's just me. If I want honesty; I ask a family member or good friend. There are a few good ones. Of that I am sure. It's just hard to know which is which sometimes. I think my head's going to explode!

Apparently, when Rosenstein found out that our wonderful President tried to blame Rosenstein for our President's decision to let Comey go, Rosenstein threatened to resign. At least this is what the original story was. This has since been recanted. Either way, this is some juicy stuff. Meanwhile, the President is back at the White House entertaining not one, but two Russian officials, Sergey Lavrov (Russia's foreign minister) and Sergey Kislyk (the Russian Ambassador to the U.S.).

A lousy 48 hours later and once again the story changed. It's so hard to keep up with the lies coming out of this White House. Now Trump says the decision to fire Comey was his and his alone and that he'd been thinking about it for a long while. My question? Why did he ever hire him in the first place?

What I find so fascinating about all of this is the total hypocrisy. Supposedly, people refused to vote for

Hillary because she told too many lies. Although my ears and statistics have proven that Trump has lied approximately five times more often than Hillary ever did; his true-blue followers will continue to make excuses for him and find ways to justify his lies by saying things like "he's flexible" or "he just changed his mind". Why didn't they give those same considerations to Hillary who "changed her mind" far less? I'm so confused. Then again, confusion is a general state of mind for me. I'm pretty used to it. So, let's just carry on, shall we?

SHUT THE FRONT DOOR! So much for just moving on, I guess. Our president may just get himself impeached before I ever get this book completed. Darn it all. He's going to kill my book sales. I think I've had to come back to this same chapter four times already. Oh well, so long as the news keeps changing; I guess my book will too. So just bear with me, ok?

Sure, I fully expected Trump to get impeached sooner rather than later; but not this soon. This has got to be a record. According to information given to the FBI and CIA and then leaked to the Washington Post; the President in all his wisdom, decided to share classified information with the Russians (Lavrov and Kislyk) while they were visiting the day after he fired Comey.

I just finished listening to General McMaster, someone I usually have a great deal of respect for, explain to the press how Trump did not say anything inappropriate; but would not actually say whether or not the material was classified. The President can declassify as he sees fit. Sadly, with this President this is very unnerving to many people, including myself. When asked who leaked the information to the Post; it almost sounded like he was saying that the Press should be able to find the leaks easier than the National Security Administration. I found that very troubling.

At the same time, I too am very concerned with all the leaks. I would also like to know where they are coming from. I want to know the truth. It's important. If the White House is being leaked, we need to know why and by whom. We need copies of those tapes. Please for God's sake do not blame it on President Obama. I am so tired of hearing him being blamed time after time after time for every little thing that goes wrong. I don't ever recall a President that took so many shots at the former president as Trump does toward Obama. It's truly a disgrace and makes our country look weak and foolish. I wish our President would stand up and accept responsibility for his own actions occasionally. Possibly even apologize.

Can you imagine? That would be something, wouldn't it? The only time he apologized was after the bus incident and that was only because he knew he was going to lose the nomination if he didn't. After five years of harassing President Obama about his birth certificate, once he finally acknowledged that Obama was indeed a citizen; he still couldn't force himself to apologize. It clearly goes against his nature. I want someone in the White House who has honor and accountability. Those are qualities crucial to the Commander-in-Chief of this country.

Why is this so important? It turns out that Comey keeps written records of certain meetings. It seems that one of the times he felt it was necessary to keep a written memo of his meeting with Trump just happened to be when he was having dinner with Trump right after Trump fired Michael Flynn.

Apparently, Trump told Comey regarding Flynn, "He's a good guy. I hope you can let this go". Uh oh! That was a "no no". This could be seen as an obstruction of justice and punishable by law, either by imprisonment or by impeachment. Apparently, nobody seems to agree if a sitting President can be indicted. Some are saying "yes", others "no". Go figure! Why do we have laws if nobody can understand them? This is way too deep for me. I'll let the professionals figure that one out.

As for the memos, there are apparently others. Comey will no doubt be asked to present them to the committee investigating Flynn and possibly Russia. Whether or not the public will see them will depend on what relevance they have and if they should be considered classified. What a freakin' mess! Fascinating, isn't it? If he was truly trying to get Comey to end the investigation into Flynn; this is a criminal offense and punishable by law.

Here's the kicker though. Most of his supporters are still going to defend him just as the Republicans are and I'll tell you why. He is a businessman, not a politician. He didn't know any better. You know what? I don't care. We are entering dangerous territory. Everybody and their mother now wants to throw their hat into the ring. Movie stars, TV stars, singers and probably dog walkers for all I know are now trying to run for President. This is crazy. Just because you like politics or you want to shake things up, doesn't mean you have a place as President of the United States. We may not always LIKE our politicians, but we still NEED them.

As I have expressed to my family and friends from time to time, I view politicians a lot like medication. You may not like it, but you need it to help keep you alive or at least make you feel better. The same holds true for Washington. Politicians are far from perfect and we need to shake it up, but they are a necessary evil. They know how to get things done. Of course, that would mean that they would have to do their job, but that's a whole different matter.

Our current President thinks he can either bully or negotiate his way through office. Guess what? Not gonna happen folks! He has put our country at great risk. Our allies don't know what to think of us and our enemies are clearly laughing at us and ready for war. Trump is not bothered. This is serious and should not be scoffed at by anyone. I don't care what side of the aisle you're on. We are all Americans. On this, we should all agree. This shouldn't be a partisan issue. We should all want the best for the country and to have good relations with our allies and at least keep a cool head with our enemies. Can't we at least find some kind of common ground on that much?

While I have admitted that I am not a big fan of our president, I will say that once Mr. Trump won the election, I was truly hoping he would prove me wrong. I wanted him to succeed. I would much rather see him succeed than have the right to say, "I told you so". After all, if our President fails, so does our country. I did not want our country to fail.

After only a mere four months into his presidency, things are extremely bleak. In case you're wondering (and I'm sure you're just dying to know), I began to write this book on May 8th. The first thing I did was think of the title because I wanted something catchy that would hopefully attract people to my book.

I'm telling you this only because things are moving so quickly right now in the world of politics that I'm afraid that by the time I finish this thing; it might belong in the 'Ancient History" Section. I HATED history.

Today's revolution (May 17th, 2017) is that Rod Rosenstein has decided to appoint a special counsel to run the FBI probe into the Trump Campaign's possible collusion involving the election as well as anything pertaining to it, including the Russian connections. Like I said, he could very well be impeached before I finish my book. Who knows? Possibly not. I had initially named the book "From the White House to the Big House". I thought the title would attract a larger number of people.

After much consideration however, I decided to change the title to avoid chasing away all the Republican readers as I believe this book is for them as well and I don't want them to think it's just another book trashing Trump. Believe it or not, I truly am trying to bring both sides together. I believe it's possible to dislike a candidate or, in this case, a president, and still find common ground and things to agree on with the other side. Am I just dreaming? I do nap often. If I don't grow on you within the next two chapters, I suggest you donate the book to Goodwill. It's for a good cause after all.

If I seem harsh on the Trump supporters, let me explain. I don't blame the supporters themselves. I do however, blame the conservative news and Trump himself. After all, if you truly want to believe in the President is that really such a bad thing? Of course not. We should want to believe in our President. The fact that I don't, doesn't mean that I blame those of you who do. I happen to respect everyone's right to have a difference of opinion.

What I find fault with is this idea that every time the news covers Trump and he doesn't like what the coverage is about; it's automatically labeled "Fake News". Not until this campaign have I heard this term used toward our press. For the past year or more; it's used almost constantly. Our President has a very contentious relationship with the press and it isn't good for the country.

On the other side, we have the conservative news stations who simply refuse to report any news story that may not shine a good light on our President. Rather than trying to clean it up (since they would have to literally lie); they instead choose to refuse to report the story altogether. This means that people that only watch stations like Fox, for instance, aren't even hearing half the news that relates to

Trump because it's bad. All they hear is the good stuff.

The President is constantly acting like he is a "victim" of the press. No other President has been treated so very, very badly. REALLY? Maybe no other President has treated the press with such disrespect. If he wants the press to treat him with respect, maybe he should return the favor. Of course, I'm just a silly girl. I don't know that much.

It is obvious to me at least, that when President Trump is asked to give a speech; he has no idea of proper etiquette. When he first spoke at the Baptist church, instead of giving an inspiring speech about the Lord, he instead chose to speak about the size of the crowds and the electoral votes until the minister interrupted him. When speaking in front of the Memorial Wall at the FBI, same thing. Just yesterday when giving the commencement speech for a class of Coast Guard grads; he chose to speak about how badly he's been treated by the press and what a witch-hunt the whole mess is. It's all about Trump. The man is all brass, no class. How rude! These men and women are getting ready to possibly go to war for our country and he's whining about his problems with the press. This is disgraceful no matter how you slice it.

He claims to love our military. Do you remember what he said during the campaign? I do. "Nobody loves the military more than I do". My memory stinks, but I remember that. I must say I'm actually glad he doesn't love me. I don't care HOW much money he has. I may be broke, but at least the people that love me are sincere.

He speaks incessantly about all the work he has accomplished during his first 100 days in office, but I fail to see it. I'm trying, but I just don't get it. I have never seen a President that has hit the campaign trail immediately after being elected into office. Maybe I just haven't been paying attention, but it seems very strange to me. It would be like me interviewing for a job and then rather than DOING the job after being hired, just consistently going to the manager's office to re-interview each day rather than work.

He hasn't passed one piece of legislation yet. Healthcare is still being sorted out in the Senate for what that's worth; his wall is now the taxpayers' responsibility and not yet started to my knowledge; the Travel Ban is still being held up in the courts; as far as the tax code goes, we do have that one-page outline basically giving the largest tax breaks to the wealthy. For anyone who may be surprised, just save it. He did exactly what he said he was going to do during his campaign. Don't you remember or did you think he was kidding? Oh sure, he has passed many executive orders. He loves to do that. He doesn't even try to get those passed through Congress, even though he has a Republican majority in both the House and Senate.

It's so much easier to be KING! Mind you, this is the man, that complained all the time about how many executive orders President Obama signed. President Trump has signed 31 executive orders after 100 days compared to President Obama's

19. Of course, President Trump has already played a minimum of 15 games of golf compared to Obama's 1 after the first 100 days. The complete hypocrisy here can't be ignored given the amount of grief D.J. gave then President Obama for golfing too often when he should have been working. This is some crazy stuff.

CHAPTER 3

Friend or Loyalist?

Do you have friends or loyalists? Until the Trump campaign, I wasn't even aware that regular people had such a thing as "loyalists". You may have noticed by now that I am not a big fan of Trump. In fact, during the campaign I used to have a phrase to describe him. I called him Teflon Don. No matter what he did or said, how terrible it sounded or seemed, his loyalists blindly followed. Nothing seemed to stick. Hence, the nickname.

I happen to have respect for the office of the presidency. Therefore, I have tried to refrain from using this term now that Trump has become the

President of the United States. It's hard not to call him names sometimes; but I try my best to show as much restraint as I possibly can. I am always successful? Not by a long shot, but I try.

So, what is the difference you may ask between a loyalist and a friend? Maybe it's not a question I am fully qualified to answer since I don't have any loyalists. However, I do have friends. This is my take on it. I love my friends and they love me (at least most do). That said, I fully expect my friends to tell me when I've made a stupid mistake or to hopefully give me their honest opinion when I ask for it; even if it hurts sometimes. If I do something stupid, especially if I hurt someone; I fully expect to be called out on my crap. That's what a real friend does. I do not want someone to tell me what I WANT to hear. I need a friend to tell me what I NEED to hear, even if it stings.

Loyalists are different from what I can tell. While I cannot go so far as to say that I admire Trump for pretty much anything; I will admit that I do marvel at the way he has with people. His "followers" are true to a fault. During his campaign, I couldn't help but notice that he never mentioned his friends. He referred to them as "loyalists". I thought that was weird to be honest.

Who doesn't have friends? I don't think Trump thinks of people the way normal people do. I think he thinks of them as commodities. He uses them for whatever he can get from them. It may be money or it may be votes or in his case many times, it's sheer admiration. He has many narcissistic characteristics.

Whoa! I'm sure that's shocking to many of you, ha? He thrives on the constant love and attention of the public. God forbid anyone should say anything bad about him. That's why he watches all the late-night TV shows and he's on Twitter so much. He needs to know what people are saying about him. If it's bad, look out. A Twitter Storm's a comin'.

Not since the days of Jim Jones have I seen this many people so eager to follow someone so blindly. From the day he first majestically rode down that golden escalator at Trump Towers until now, people have been fascinated with him. No matter whether he offends Mexicans by calling many of them illegals, rapists and murderers or even mocking a disabled journalist, nothing bothers them. Even when they released the tape from Access Hollywood with him speaking to Billy Bush about the things he likes to do to women and bragging about how he gets away with it…nothing! Several women came forward after that tape was released and told their stories of being sexually harassed by Trump.

What do you suppose happened to all those women? They just suddenly disappeared. If you ask a Trump supporter, I'm sure they'll tell you it's because they were all lying. I think otherwise. I see a presidential candidate with a boatload of money to spend and a non-disclosure agreement somewhere.

Those women didn't have nearly the monetary resources to fight that Trump did. That's just a guess on my part. I just find it strange that they so suddenly disappeared off the face of the map at the same time another batch of Hillary's emails were released. It shifted the focus off Trump right back to Hillary all over again. Even when Trump stood up and literally said something like, "Russia, if you're listening, if you can find Hillary's missing 33,000 emails; I'm sure you will be mightily rewarded by the American Press".

Republicans all over still protected him by stating it was a joke. Do you honestly think that they would have thought it was a joke if Obama had said something like that? Obama at least had a good sense of humor. Trump is just a mean guy and a bully. He's not that funny. Let's get real here. Even if he did mean it as a joke; what are the odds that Russia took it that way? Do you really believe it's just a coincidence that all those emails were leaked not long afterward? You can always make the argument that it doesn't matter how they were received; it only matters what they showed. You're right. Let's think about that for a moment, shall we? The emails that were released were the same emails that had already been reviewed by the FBI.

So why did these emails affect the election? They put doubt in the minds of the people who were still on the fence as to who to vote for; that's how. We have no way of ever knowing if the election results would have been different if those emails had not been leaked because there is no way to get into someone's head and tell if they would have changed their mind.

A recall election would not have helped. The seeds of doubt had already been planted. Trump won the campaign by the electoral vote. Whether we like it or not, a fact is a fact. We will never know if Hillary could have won if she had spent more time in the blue-collar states or if the emails had not been re-investigated by Comey. I think the one thing we can all agree on is that it was probably the dirtiest campaign in recent history.

Was Trump totally responsible for the dirty campaign? Of course not! I do believe that Hillary really did start out trying to stick to policy, but it didn't take too long before she was down in the mud right along with him. I can't say I blame her necessarily, although I still say it was a bad move. It was hard not to comment on some of the things he said and did. She took the bait. I wish she had spent that energy going to more of the blue-collar states and listening more to what people there had to say about their jobs and what they were afraid of rather than just talking about taxes, wages and making education cheaper. While these are surely very important issues to most of us, for a lot of Americans, jobs are number one. Why didn't she just listen to Bill? Oh wait! I know. Women NEVER listen to their husbands. That's why. Don't get too giddy guys. You know darned well you don't listen to us either. Gee, and we wonder why the divorce rate is so high!

While I don't think she was the best candidate; I still think she is an intelligent woman extremely capable of being President of this country. At first, I was too busy being angry at the Democrats for basically pushing her on us; but as time went by I came to know her better and began to understand her. I started liking her. Learning about how much of her youth and college years was spent helping people less fortunate than her, truly impressed me. She became more humanized. I learned more about the Benghazi incident and how tragic it was. I learned her part in it and how long it took her to clear her name. I could never do a job like that. I think it's very easy for the rest of us to armchair quarterback her actions in Benghazi.

How many of us have jobs where one misstep or misunderstanding could cause somebody's life? I don't know how people in those positions do it. I don't care if it's a Democrat, a Republican, a Libertarian, or an Independent. I have a great deal of compassion for anyone holding these positions. That includes Rex Tillerson. I may not care for his personality, but I don't have to. I just have to respect the job he's doing. We don't see much respect anymore, do we? Where do you suppose it went? I'll cover that in another chapter. Onward and Upward!

This Page Intentionally Left Blank

CHAPTER 4

IS ANYONE LISTENING?

Has anyone noticed that nobody seems to be listening to one another anymore? Oh sure, they text, they Facebook, they tweet, on rare occasions they might even make the magnanimous gesture of actually speaking to someone on the phone; but how often do we really LISTEN? We seem to either talk AT or PAST each other. It has never been more apparent than it has been in the past decade or so.

I put most of the blame on social media, but I'm an old person so what do I know? I used to like it when people actually sat across from each other and spoke and heard each other out. This is no longer the case. We text and wait for a written reply possibly hours or even days later. What the heck? I hate that! Did I happen to mention that I'm old? Sorry, I don't mean to repeat myself, but it bears repeating. I really, really, hate that.

When it comes to politics, look out! Nobody is even allowed to have a different opinion anymore. You are either on MY side or you're WRONG... PERIOD! Families are feuding and friendships are tearing apart all because of politics. It was bad enough during the Obama Administration.

In fact, I couldn't believe how much disrespect people were willing to show toward a sitting president. I'd never seen or heard anything quite like it. I'm all for the Freedom of Speech, but let's get something straight. No matter what you may think of the man holding that office, he or she is still Commander in Chief of this country. As such, they are due a certain amount of respect.

When I heard that President Obama was referred to as a Monkey and later compared to Hitler by one of our lovely Arizona Congresswomen; I nearly lost it. They even took shots at Michelle by calling her an "Ape in High Heels". For anyone who thinks this is perfectly ok and falls under the Amendment covering Free Speech, I just have one thing to say. Shame on you! Racist remarks like these are NEVER ok when referring to ANYBODY, let alone a President and First Lady.

As I said earlier, when Trump first began his campaign I used to call him Teflon Don. Since then, although I do not like the man or what he stands for, I have tried my best to refrain from any name calling (at least not in public). What I might do in the privacy of my own home is a different story. I'll never tell.

I will openly admit that during the Bush years, I was not a happy camper. I hated the idea of going to war with Saddam Hussein. To be honest, I didn't feel that George W was cut out to be President. That said, I always thought he was an honorable man and a wonderful family man. I still do. I could separate the man from the office. I used to tell people that I always thought he'd be a blast to have a barbecue with, even if he was a lousy President in my eyes. Why do people think it's ok to belittle a person's character based simply on the job they hold? I feel differently about Trump sadly. I felt the same way about him long before he ever ran for President. My feelings about his him have not as much to do with the job, as they do with his character.

Let's get back to the problem of communication for a bit. How do you think we can fix this problem? For me it's simple. I hate my stupid cell phone. I couldn't care less if I get a text. I'd much rather to talk to someone; but that's me. I do recognize that I'm stuck in my old ways and most people are not like me. Here's a thought. If I had teenagers at home, I might try something small like this. This is not me being smart (God forbid). I've seen this on TV. Yeah, I watch a lot of TV. Why not try asking everyone (including mom and dad) to put their cell phones down during all meals. Have real conversations at the dinner table and don't give the cell phones back until the last person is done eating. Of course, if there's an emergency, adjustments can always be made; but at least it's a start.

At night when everyone goes to bed, the cell phones go to bed too. Place them in a bowl or someplace safe in mom and dad's room where the kids can't get to them. After all, if the kid's supposed to be sleeping, they shouldn't be getting phone calls anyway. As for the adults, let's try this. If you go out to eat with your friends or even your spouse or a date or whatever; try putting your phone in your pocket or your purse and not answering it. Just let the calls go to voicemail. Unless you have small children at home and your babysitter is calling; let it go. Try having a real face to face conversation. You might actually enjoy it and it will give your thumbs a break too.

As for the rest of it, why can't we all just agree to disagree? People all have a right to their own opinions. Those opinions should be valued. Just because you don't share another person's point of view doesn't mean that you shouldn't at least respect it. Listen to what they say. If you're smart, you might even learn something. If you immediately tune them out, you will never learn anything about that person or their logic. You're the loser, not them. You may not agree, but at least give them a chance to tell you why they feel the way they do.

It's perfectly ok to get into a heated discussion occasionally. After all, we're only human. I enjoy it. Just don't go too close to the edge. You might not be able to come back.

By now you are obviously thinking I'm a total genius. Yepper! Let's go with that. Now for my next words of wisdom. By now you must be boiling over with anticipation. I'll try not to disappoint you.

CHAPTER 5

THE PRES AND THE PRESS

Do you remember way back when? You know what I mean. During the campaign, our now President Trump had a virtual love affair with the American Press. Heck, they pretty much helped him win the election. Oh sure, most of the news was negative, but since when does that matter? Any news is good news.

The rest of the Republican candidates received little to no press coverage. Why? Because the press was absolutely fascinated with the antics of Donald J. Trump. The more outrageous he became; the more coverage he got. He lapped it up like a kitten with a bowl of milk.

So, what the heck happened? For one thing, I don't think anybody, including Trump himself, except for maybe a few, actually envisioned him winning the election. After all, poll after poll all showed that Hillary had an extensive lead. Suddenly, the press started taking things a little more seriously and began reporting the facts and not just Trump's crazy antics. It all started with the size of the inaugural crowd.

Frankly, I never thought it was fair to even compare the size of his crowd to Obama's. After all, President Obama was the first black man to have ever been elected President of this country. It only stands to reason that his crowd would be the largest. So why even go there? But Trump was mad as Hell! He insisted that his crowd was the biggest crowd in history. They had pictures and they even had ticket counters, but that still didn't satisfy him. He just had to show the world that he had the biggest crowd size. If it was only for a few days or so and then he'd dropped it, so be it; but no. He is still talking about to this day. He is like a little boy bragging that "my toys are better than your toys". He is so childlike that I worry for our country.

Most recently, he locked the American Press out of the meetings with Sergey Lavrov and Sergey Kesnyk while allowing the Russians inside. Say what?? Before that, he has been known to accuse the press of printing FAKE NEWS every time they print a story he doesn't feel is flattering to him. He berates reporters and calls them names. He makes up pseudonyms for various news programs. While being interviewed by John Dickerson of Face the Nation recently, he even had the nerve to tell John that he liked the show even though he called it "DEface the Nation". Talk about rude. When John Dickerson asked him if he still believed that Obama had Trump Towers surveilled, Trump merely dismissed him.

As a result, Stephen Colbert nearly got himself fired from his Late-Night TV Program after coming to John's defense with a rather off-color joke. I love Stephen Colbert, but he really did go a little too far that time. I don't think he deserves to be fired however. His show is after 10:30 pm. Kids shouldn't be watching anyway. At least I hope not.

Now let's talk a little bit about Sean Spicer. At first, I honestly couldn't stand the guy. He just seemed to be so darned rude to the reporters. These are the same men and women that he has worked alongside with for years. Now he's snapping at them and won't let them finish their questions and acting like a real jerk.

My opinion of him has changed over time. I'm just afraid it might be too late. I have a feeling he's about to get a letter from the President when he's away from his desk (get it?).

My reason? For one, he looks like a heart attack waiting to happen. I don't care if I like him or not; I really don't want anybody to die of a heart attack, ok? He is so stressed every day that he approaches that podium; I feel sorry for the guy. Think about it. Every morning when he wakes up, his first thought must be "Oh my God, what did he tweet last night and how am I going to clean up this mess?". This guy must defend the indefensible each and every day.

On top of that, he can never be sure if the President is going to change gears and tell another story in a couple hours. Then Sean will have go back out there and try to explain why the first story was true, but so is the second one; just different. YIKES! I wonder how many aspirin he takes a day? I know he chews a lot of gum. I hope it's sugarless. If not, his dentist must be rich.

Lately, I notice we've been seeing more of the Deputy Press Secretary, Sarah Huckabee Sanders. I have a bad feeling that she will be the next Press

Secretary to replace Sean. She's a real charmer. If I thought Sean was rude; look out for this one. She looks very innocent (like a cute little church lady almost) in her cardigan sweaters; but don't let that fool you. Listen to her words. She's mean as a snake. Maybe my opinion of her will change too. We'll see. She's the daughter of Governor Mike Huckabee. Who knew?

Since the story has been changing ever so quickly regarding Comey's firing, the President has now tweeted that perhaps he will just stop having press briefings. His excuse? Well, apparently, he is just so darned fast moving that he doesn't have the time to keep his subordinates all updated on the facts which is why they occasionally report the wrong information. Hmmm..ok. I'm sure it's because he's so busy passing all that legislation. No wait, he hasn't done that yet. Or maybe he's busy getting the wall paid for by Mexico. No. That's not happening. Or maybe he's busy working with Congress on the tax code. No, not yet.

Healthcare? I haven't heard anything from the Senate yet, have you? Foreign Affairs? We'll discuss what I think of that whole mess in a bit. From what I can tell, this President is actually the least busy President we've ever had. He spends most of his time entertaining dignitaries (that's work I suppose) and golfing on the weekends. The rest of the time he is on twitter or watching TV.

He has a lot of time on his hands apparently. More than any President I've ever known anyway. How does he do that? I know he doesn't sleep much. A lot of elderly people don't require much sleep and I'm sure he's one of them. Let's not forget, he is 70 after all. Now he does sign a whole lot of executive orders. If I were to venture a guess, I would say that at least 70% of them were merely a reversal of something President Obama passed. Trump has shown Obama so much disdain and contempt, it's hurtful to watch.

I have never seen another President treat the President before him in such a disgusting way. His sole purpose seems to be to undo anything that Obama did. It doesn't matter if it hurts the country or not as long as it unravels something Obama passed. Trump isn't here to make America Great Again. He's only here to Break America, at least as I see it. He does love a good rally however. Have you noticed that he seldom speaks to crowds with both supporters and dissenters? I haven't. He's far more comfortable throwing a rally than he is in reaching out to those who didn't vote for him originally. He simply doesn't have any interest in us. I understand that many of you have different opinions. That's perfectly ok. We're all good here.

For those of you who are so impressed with the fact that this President refused to take a salary; perhaps you should think of it this way. The guy's a multimillionaire. The President's salary is only $400,000 per year. That's like giving him pocket change. One weekend trip to Mara Lago has already taken up that entire year's salary and a whole lot more.

According to the Washington Post and the Washington Watchdog, both estimate that each trip costs the American taxpayer 3 million dollars. Considering how many times he's made that trip now, I'd say he's gotten his salary and then some, wouldn't you? Must be nice. I can't complain however.

I went to Florida twice myself. Of course, I stayed with my Aunt and Uncle. It was very nice though. It sure didn't cost 3 million. Then again, nobody was watching my body. Wait, that didn't sound right. Moving on!

This Page Intentionally Left Blank

CHAPTER 6

HAS ANYONE SEEN THE MIDDLE CLASS?

For as long as I can remember, the middle class has always supported both the upper and lower classes with their hard-earned tax dollars. Sadly, this is still true. Unfortunately, the middle class is beginning to shrink to a level that is now dangerously low and it will no longer be able to sustain the weight of the world on its' shoulders.

For far too long, Washington has been taxing the heck out of the middle class to make the rich richer and to barely help the poor to the point that now half the middle class is now part of the lower class, meaning that only a few middle-class families are left to carry the burden. FEAR NOT! This past November 2016, our country voted for a multi-billionaire to become President of the United States. The hope is that he will bring his business expertise to the White House and therefore, create jobs, strengthen the economy and lower taxes for the lower and middle classes. REALLY??

Could we please think this through for a minute? This is a man who has had no political or military experience in his life. What were you guys thinking? Didn't you notice that while he had his thumbs up in the air, he also had his first and second fingers crossed? He's a super-rich businessman who suddenly wants to help the little guy by "draining the swamp" of Wall Street. GOOD JOB YOU! Aside from

Generals Mattis and McMaster, and perhaps Nikki Haley; I have pretty much no respect for any of the multi-millionaires he has appointed to his now shark filled cabinet. Dude! Again, how were the supposed Wall Street people that you were supposed to be draining the swamp of any worse than sharks?

Hell, we've gone from the Apprentice to Shark Tank in less than 80 days. Several of them are already under investigation for various things, but we'll get into that later. Of course, he still has plenty of room to fill so to his credit, there's still a chance some less fortunate people may still make the cut. Let's keep the faith. My head is already hurting and I'm only getting started. Are you guys ok? I sure hope so. If not, just take a short break. I promise it will get better.

Let's see what's he's done for the middle class so far, shall we? This book is being started right around the 105th day of the presidency, so of course much of this could change by the time this book ever gets read, so please be patient. Remember, I'm a newbie.

We've just gotten the Republicans' Healthcare bill passed by the House. Trump did such a victory dance you would have thought he'd just built another Trump Tower. Sadly, most Americans, both Democrat and Republican are not very happy with this bill as it now stands. Most people don't even know what the bill covers or how much premiums or deductibles will be, but we are all supposed to celebrate the "death" of Obamacare.

Why is that? Because it's NOT Obamacare and Trump said it's better.

We should believe him. In all my years of living, if there is one thing I've learned, if someone tells you "believe me", run the other way. Unless someone can show you the goods and just expects you to believe them because they say so; don't fall for it. NOT GONNA HAPPEN!

What we do know so far is that the states will have the option to opt out of certain healthcare that was previously guaranteed under Obamacare. For instance, there are an entire page of pre-existing conditions that will now be left up to each individual state to decide whether they want to cover or not. Just some of these include the following:

- Acne
- Alzheimer's Disease
- Ambulance
- Anemia

- Anxiety
- Arthritis
- Asthma
- Bipolar disease
- Cancer
- Cardiomyopathy
- Cerebral Palsy (infantile)
- Chronic Obstructive Pulmonary Disease
- Cystic Fibrosis
- Depression
- Diabetes
- Dialysis
- Menstrual irregularities
- Multiple Sclerosis
- Muscular Dystrophy
- Obesity
- Paraplegia
- Parkinson's Disease
- Pregnancy
- Renal Failure
- Scleroderma
- Sleep Apnea
- Tuberculosis

This is only a partial list of what is expected to be presented to 13 very white Senators for consideration according to several reports by ABC

News with David Muir and CNN. Please note that several of these conditions are strictly applicable to women only. Cystic Fibrosis is most commonly found in the African American community.

I couldn't help but notice that erectile dysfunction was not listed. Gee, that's odd. How does a woman get punished for being pregnant or having irregular menstrual cycles and yet a man does not get held to that same standard? There should be at the very least, two women and two people of color on this panel to give fair representation to all.

Yet there is not one Black Senator or one woman placed on this 13-member panel to make some of the most important decisions that affect our daily lives. This is hardly worthy of a black-tie event. At least not in my view.

Let's see how well the Senate can clean this up. I am hoping for the best, but not necessarily hopeful.

This entire Healthcare issue seems to be all wrapped up in saving the Government money without raising taxes on the rich. For myself personally, I will not have to worry too much unless the money comes from Medicare. I do however worry about my grandchildren and children. Both of my granddaughters have pre-existing conditions. I hate the idea that for the rest of their adult lives they will be punished for having problems that are out of their control. I know what it's like.

I have more PRE-existing conditions than NON-existing conditions. I went a full year, after I took an early retirement due to illness, without any medical insurance. I tried to get private insurance but was denied coverage for a whole list of reasons including menopause of all things. This was just before the ACA became law and not too long before I turned 65 and became eligible for Medicare. Thank you, Medicare! Before I was flat out denied, I was given quotes of around $500 a month with a $10,000 deductible. That's right. You heard me correctly. Even with a $10,000 deductible my premium would have been around $500.00.

They still denied me coverage stating I had pre-existing conditions. Mind you, none of these conditions are in any way life threatening or even that costly to treat. If only Obamacare had been available to me at that time, I could have had coverage. With my low income, I would have been eligible for a large subsidy and my premiums would have been much lower. Yes, I get it. It certainly wasn't perfect. The premiums were too high as were the deductibles.

I'm sure there were a lot of other things as well. Please just bear with me for a moment while I try to explain in layman's terms (at least to the best of my understanding) what happened to the original ACA before we ended up with the final product which was then tagged Obamacare.

I am no expert in the field of medicine, but I did spend much of my career paying medical claims, so I guess that means I have a little bit of an edge understanding insurance over the "average bear". That my friends, is a direct quote from the famous scholar Yogi Bear. Most of you probably aren't even old enough to remember him, but

I am. I forget what my kids' names are sometimes, but at least I remember Yogi Bear. Hey! That's just how I roll.

I'm sure many of you are familiar with all the screaming that has been done about the big lie that President Obama told when he promised that people would be able to keep their own insurance if they wanted rather than take the ACA. Remember? That provision was called the Public Option, of which there had been three different types. The president pushed for this, but by the time the bill finally made it to the Senate, they voted it down allowing instead for the insurance companies to have a larger piece of the pie.

I was working for one of the largest insurance companies at the time the ACA was being drafted. I will not name the company, but I will tell you that we were basically given a "gentle reminder" that a vote for Obama could very well mean the end of our jobs if his healthcare act went through.

Once the bill was in the Senate, within a matter of weeks our newsletter came out with a nice big picture of our CEO shaking hands with the President of the United States and an article talking about how great it was that the insurance companies could come to an agreement with Congress to get this legislation passed. I must admit, I think I threw up in my mouth just a little bit. I was so upset with President Obama for making that concession. I knew he had to do it just to get it off the ground, but it still angered me.

Instead of calling it Obamacare, we should have called it Congress Care. Once the President realized that the Republicans weren't going to cooperate with him no matter what he proposed; he handed the bill over to Congress and basically told them "fine, you tell how you'd like it and we'll do it". The Republicans and insurance companies put their heads together and came up with their own plan; the president made a few changes and the rest is history.

Either way, this is no way the original bill that President Obama had presented to Congress. If the Public Option had been left in; people could have opted to keep their own coverage if they wanted. At least that's my understanding of the whole thing and that's why the former President is still being accused of lying. It's too bad because he wasn't lying. He just had to negotiate with Congress to get the bill passed. I wasn't happy when he did that, but I understood it. I don't imagine he was very happy about it either, but what do I know?

What's different between our former and current president is this. President Obama did not lay blame on Congress for the public option or the shortcomings of the ACA. When the Republicans began to tag it Obamacare in the hope to detract voters, he never once complained. He accepted the name Obamacare and accepted full responsibility for both its' successes and its' failures.

In fact, President Obama never tried to lay blame on anyone that I can recall, but maybe I just missed it. I miss a lot of stuff! I guess I've just always admired the fact that he has always held his head high and accepted full responsibility for his own actions. I miss that.

Now for tax reform. Did someone say tax reform? While the middle and lower class that voted for him were hoping he would be putting money in their pocket, they may just be a little disappointed. The Republican Party has for the most part at least, always believed in "trickle-down" economics.

Over my lifetime, I've seen this wonderful concept used more than once and each time it is a temporary fix at best. The concept behind it is supposed to create jobs and stimulate the economy by having the wealthiest spending their money here in the U.S. rather than abroad. The biggest problem as I see it is that the rich don't generally take that money and SPEND it here in the good old USA. The smart ones take it and INVEST it. That's how they manage to not only STAY rich, but get richer. In no way does this stimulate the economy of the United States.

President Trump wants to lower taxes on companies like his own claiming that this will allow them to pay their employees more in salaries and again stimulate the economy. Oh, he's so darned silly sometimes. I mean really? I've worked for both small companies as well as giant corporations and let me tell you something. Nothing compares to the greed of the corporate world.

Do you really think these Corporate giants are going to take those extra tax dollars and give their employees an extra 5% on top of their usual 2% annual salary increase? I think there's a far bigger chance that these Corporations are more likely to take that extra money and give the CEO's, CFO's, COO's and whatever other Coocoo's there are out there some nice big bonuses. But hey! They are used to being rich, so they need it more to maintain their current lifestyles.

The poor are used to being poor. I think that's the way we're supposed to look at it. If they throw us a crumb, we should be grateful and shut up. After all, it's better than nothing. Don't get me wrong, there are many advantages to working for a big corporation, but they are still greedy for the most part. There are of course, exceptions. Some corporations are known to be very generous with their employees. It just depends on the company.

So, what do we do to fix the economy? Well, beats the heck out of me. I can barely handle my own measly little budget. When I say little; I mean miniscule. I basically go to the store to buy a package of hamburger, some toilet paper, milk and laundry soap and my money's gone. Now THAT'S what you call an easy budget. I'm guessing the country's economy might be a little rougher. That's why we have brilliant businessmen like Trump in the White House to figure it all out on one piece of paper. Sheesh! I have another migraine. Sorry! Next......

CHAPTER 7

FRIENEMIES?

What do you make of an American President who seems to be Hell bent on making nice with our enemies more than he's concerned with maintaining good relationships with our allies? I simply do not understand.

On the one hand, I understand the importance of trying to establish some sort of relationship with those that are not allies. It's important that we can come to agreements on trade and matters of national security. I get it, ok? But since when do you deliberately push your allies aside in favor of those who have wronged us consistently?

That's simply not a good strategy, no matter how you slice it.

Let's put it this way. If I have a group of friends who have always been good to me and loved me like a sister, am I going to desert them to try to establish a friendship with someone who has been mean to me for years (possibly decades) just because I need something from them? I don't think so. I trust my old friends far more than I am going to trust a new friend that was most recently an adversary. It simply doesn't make sense.

Let's just start with Putin since it seems that our president's entire cabinet is somehow involved with Russia in one way or another. We'll know more of course, once the investigations are over. In the meantime, I keep picturing Trump and

Putin riding bareback on a horse into the sunset. Of course, Putin will have his tanned bare chest and I envision Trump with reddish gold hair flowing off his fatty back. Ok, that was mean. I apologize. You must admit the visual is pretty funny though.

Then we have Kim Jong Un from North Korea. Now there's someone you most definitely shouldn't mess with. This guy is scary with a capital "S". Trump once referred to him as "one smart cookie". He sounded like he admires this man. NO, WE DON'T! I refer to him as Fu Man Coo- Coo. That guy's a looney tune. We don't admire loose cannons nor do we try to be friends. Yes, we can try to maintain some sort of co-existence; but that's as far as it goes. OY! North Korea is by far the country we should fear the most. They are currently testing missiles capable of reaching the U.S. and they have nuclear weapons. Coo-Coo is nuts. We don't like him. Maybe Tillerson needs to remind the president with little sticky notes which leaders we like and which ones we don't.

I sincerely think he's losing it. I am genuinely serious. Let's face it. The man is 70 years old and being president is the most difficult job there is. That job ages every man who has ever held that position. Why is it so hard to believe that it would have an even faster effect on someone who's already 70? I truly believe he's starting to show signs of dementia.

I'm only 68 and I couldn't do that job. Heck, there are jobs much easier than that, that I couldn't do. I'm not even commenting on his intellect (I could, but I won't). I am simply stating that he could have a medical condition that is affecting his cognitive abilities. If so, he should not be holding the highest office in the land.

Recently, Trump went to Saudi Arabia and played nice there, too. What? After all the terrible things he's been saying about the Muslims and his Travel Ban still in the courts he now wants to cozy up to Saudi? Gee, do you think money has anything to do with it? After all, he's still got his hotels there you know. We seem to forget that this White House is loaded with conflicts of interest, remember?

According to the Washington Post, President Trump had registered 8 companies in Saudi Arabia during the 2016 campaign. Of course, he wants to play nice. I would too if I were him.

Other dictators our president seems to admire have included Rodrigo Duterte of the Philippines. Duterte has been charged with crimes against humanity and thousands of drug related deaths committed by state sponsored vigilante groups. President Trump has told President Duterte that he is doing a great job and he would like him to come to Washington to discuss North Korea.

Another frienemy, if you will, is Turkey's President Recep Tayyip Erdogan. He's a real good guy and Trump has nothing but nice things to say about him. He happens to be the President of Turkey. Since I'm not here to give you a History lesson; I won't bother. Just trust me. I wouldn't trust him to walk my dog. Then again, I happen to be an avid animal lover and probably wouldn't trust most people;

so, there's that. Erdogan however, is a real piece of work.

The most recent evidence of bad behavior on our president's part came just a few days ago when yet again, there was another terrorist attack on the London Bridge of all places. The images and stories were truly heartbreaking. The UK and Britain have been struck by terror three times within a very short period of time. How did our president respond? He chose to attack the Mayor of London for not using strong enough language. He failed to listen or read the entire message, since he quoted something entirely out of context. He does this consistently.

He really needs an editor for his tweets. Speaking of editors, where the heck is Melania? Shouldn't she be coming home soon? I sure hope so.

Maybe she can keep an eye on him. He's like a child who's constantly sneaking into the cookie jar. And this my friends, is our President. Scary, right? It is to me at least. I can't imagine how this president would handle another 9-11 situation if God forbid that should happen again.

I truly don't think he'd know where to turn. He doesn't take the advice of his advisors because he believes with all his heart that he is smarter than all of them. Yes, he has chosen Generals to be in his Cabinet, but do you recall when he once said that he was smarter than all the Generals? That happens to be one of the view times I think he was telling the truth; at least his version of it.

Another example of our president's one-sided thinking

happened just last week when sadly our president probably did the worst thing he could have done for our country and the rest of the world, not to mention the planet. He took it upon himself to pull the United States out of the Paris Climate Accord.

This was against all advice given to him by multiple corporations, his own daughter Ivanka as well as his Secretary of State, Rex Tillerson. Why you ask? Well, according to him it was for the good of the country and to keep his campaign promise. I beg to disagree. You can believe him if you want and I am sure that many of you will; but I have my own assessment. So far, this president has not passed one piece of legislation that requires congressional approval that is of any real significance. Sure, you can say that the Healthcare Act finally made it through the House, but it still hasn't made it through the Senate and they are completely rewriting it aren't they? So again, nothing.

The only things he has accomplished have been done through executive orders which do not require anyone's approval. These are all unilateral decisions. Even then, if you take a close look at these orders; they are nothing more than an unraveling of everything that President Obama put into place. President Trump has such a deep seeded hatred for Obama that he has made it his sole mission to undo everything that Obama put into place. It doesn't matter if it hurts the country or not.

He simply doesn't care as long as he can stick it to the former president. This is a travesty and that is why I am so angry. I really did want to give him a chance, but he blew it about a month in. Believe me when I tell you I take no pleasure in saying that, because I don't. We need our president to succeed or our country fails. I worry for this country. I think many of us feel the same way. This makes me very sad. I worry for my children, my grandchildren and hopefully someday my great-grandchildren.

The world stage is watching us right now to see where we go from here. Now that we have pulled out of the Paris Climate Accord, we have basically given China the number one spot in the world economically. Thank you, Mr. President. I hope your grudge was worth it. At least we will now have coal jobs, right? Just check the classifieds. I'm sure you'll find all sorts of coal related jobs. While you're at it, you may want to stockpile some coal to keep in your basement for the cold winter. I remember when I was a kid that my grandparents used to shovel the filthy stuff into their furnace to keep the house warm. Maybe we'll go back to doing that again. After all, I hear it's much cheaper. Just think of how much we're all going to save on electricity and gas. Coal is the new clean energy. YES!

Remember, I did warn you about my sarcastic sense of humor. Sometimes the sarcasm is just a little much. I'll try to contain myself. Moving on.....

CHAPTER 8

Accountability – Dead and Buried

Many of you have probably had this same conversation. I know I have with many members of my own family and friends. Nobody seems to be willing to hold themselves accountable for their own actions anymore. It's not even just the younger generations either. That I might expect. It seems to be all age groups.

Is the president responsible? No, at least not entirely. He is however, in a position that our children should be able to look up to. Sadly, he is the least responsible person I can think of. He literally dogged President Obama for five years about his citizenship. Once he was finally forced to admit that he was wrong and had to publicly admit that Obama was in fact, a United States citizen; even then he could not be bothered to say the simple words I apologize for any pain I may have caused you and your family to the president.

This president NEVER takes responsibility for anything he does wrong. He always finds someone else to blame. The very first raid into Yemen when the young soldier lost his life, rather than taking responsibility as Commander-in-Chief, instead he blamed the Generals. Come on! Really? That's just wrong. I know of no other president in our history that has ever blamed our Generals when lives are lost on the battlefield. The president is

COMMANDER-IN-CHIEF for crying out loud. They always take responsibility. Well, they used to anyway.

So, I guess my point is this. If we can't even look to the President of the United States to take responsibility, maybe it's too much to ask our kids to take responsibility for their actions, right? WRONG!

As adults, we have a duty to our children and society in general to change the way we handle ourselves. Who are the people you respect the most in this world? My guess is that it would more than likely be somebody who is honorable, truthful, kind and willing to admit they made a mistake when they accidentally step in it. Those are the people I admire the most at least. It's not always easy to apologize. It's not always easy to accept responsibility for something that goes wrong, but people will respect you more for it if you own up to your own mistakes. We all make them. Of course, in my case, I'm a pro. If there was any money in it, I'd give lessons.

In case you're thinking I only pick on the Republicans, guess again. Recently, Hillary Clinton gave an interview where she once again blamed James Comey, the Russian intervention and now even the DNC for her loss. Come on, Hillary.

Sure, we all know these things all played an important role in your loss, but we can't be certain you would have won even without that interference. Do I believe you would have? Yes, I do. However, it just sounds tacky. Just take ownership of your loss and move on. Listening to her talk about having to "fuel" the DNC with her own money really upset me. After all, most of Bernie Sanders donations were small donations from a small grass roots effort and he made a great deal of money. He didn't need the help of the DNC. God knows he didn't get it. The DNC placed all their bets on Hillary. They had no intention of letting Bernie win.

Then there's Kathy Griffin. This one runs more along the lines of disrespect for the office rather than accountability, although it can be used in both cases. She recently posted a picture of a beheaded Donald Trump. Now, I did not personally see the post, only the redacted version thankfully.

As a result of this so-called joke, she has lost her contract with CNN, several sponsors and has lost multiple bookings. Do I agree? You betcha! At least in Kathy's case she did offer a sincere apology. She acknowledged that she crossed a line she cannot come back from. I believe her apology was sincere, but not enough to save her job.

After all, if she had a job in any other industry, she'd be out of a job so fast it would make your head spin. Somehow, comedians seem to feel they can get away with the unthinkable simply because they are just being funny. Guess what? That wasn't funny. Not only wasn't it funny, it was extremely disrespectful to the leader of our country.

I may not agree with his policies or even like his personality for that matter, but he is still our president and he deserves a certain amount of respect whether I like him or not. It's just that simple.

As adults, we have a duty to our children and society in general to change the way we handle ourselves. Who are the people you respect the most in this world? My guess is that it would more than likely be somebody who is honorable, truthful, kind and willing to admit they made a mistake when they accidentally step in it.

Those are the people I admire the most at least. It's not always easy to apologize. It's not always easy to accept responsibility for something that goes wrong, but people will respect you more for it if you own up to your own mistakes. We all make them. Of course, in my case, I'm a pro. If there was any money in it, I'd give lessons.

So, who is responsible for this gradual change in our social behavior? Trump is not a good role model, that we know; but is he responsible? No. This has started well over a decade ago in my opinion. Since I'm an old fart, I like to blame everything on social media. It's just so darned easy, isn't it?

After all, nobody cares what they say or how they say it. They can be as rude as they want with no guilt. They hide behind their computer screen and pretend there isn't a real person reading those words on the other end of that post, tweet or text. It has taken all the personalization out of our conversations, leaving people to act in a way they would never normally act face to face. People have become not just mean, but angry as well due to the things they read every day. It's very sad when you think about it. It's times like this I thank God for my short-term memory. I forgot what I was talking about, so I will move on to the next chapter. Try to keep up.

This Page Intentionally Left Blank

CHAPTER 9

It's Good to Be King

On January 20, 2016 Donald J. Trump became the 45th President of the United States. While he may not have won the popular vote, he did win the electoral vote. We have heard him brag about this many, many times. He even thought about demanding a recount of the popular vote just to prove that he had won that vote as well.

Simply put, Mr. Trump is a narcissist. He needs to feel that he is loved by everyone and that he is better than everyone else. This is not a good fit for a president. This is only my highly valued opinion. Ok, let's just pretend that's the case. It's makes me feel better.

Part of this chapter will no doubt sound a little redundant and for that, I apologize; but some of this does bear repeating.

Here in this country, we elect a President to oversee the Executive Branch of our country and to serve as Commander-in-Chief of our Armed Forces. In some countries like England for instance, they have a King and a Queen. In England of course, the Royal Family is a big deal and we as Americans find them fascinating to watch. Of course, exactly what they do has always been a little bit of a mystery to me to be honest. I know they always show up for all the pomp and circumstance stuff. The Queen herself has a remarkable history and is an incredible woman in her own right. Other than that, I really don't know how their Parliament fits into the daily working of the government. I doubt if Theresa May, the Prime Minister of the UK must check with the Queen to see if it's ok to travel to a NATO meeting. Do you see where I'm coming from here? Whatever you do, do NOT use this book as a reference for a school paper, ok? I'm really not that smart. I try to keep my information as factual as I can, but I'm no genius. That, my friends, is accountability. Refer to Chapter 7.

Now, as for our current president. What do you say? President or King? I see a President who is just itching to be King. He is a God among men. All you need to do is watch him when he gives one of his "rallies". From the minute he walks onto the stage, he has his thumbs up, then the hand clapping, again more thumbs up and hand clapping and pointing to various people in the crowd. By the time he gets to the podium he stands there and holds both sides of the podium while cocking his head to the left with that big grin. Of course, there are a multitude of "thank you's" throughout his routine. After all, he does see himself as a rock star.

Almost everything he has done to date was all done by Executive Order with the exception of the Healthcare Act which is still waiting to get passed through the Senate. Even his Executive Orders were not original ideas. He basically unraveled most everything Obama did. It didn't matter if it was good or bad. It only mattered that it was something that Obama approved. It had to go. PERIOD!

Trump isn't alone in his hatred of Obama. That much is certain. I've never seen so much disrespect toward any president. Not even poor President Bush got that much disrespect and name calling. Our nation seems to have lost its' way when it comes to having respect for the office of the president, even if you don't particularly like the person who holds that office.

As I've said, I disagreed with almost everything G.W. did while president; but I was always able to separate the man from the office and I always respected the fact that he was the leader of this country. Something changed when Obama took office. People felt free to say anything they wanted. I truly believe it started with the birther movement. Yes, Trump started it, but we don't have to finish it. My distrust of Mr. Trump runs very,

very deep. He makes me fear for our country. I will respect the office, but I am really struggling. He needs to reach out to people who are not just his base. I realize he appreciates loyalty and that's why he only cares about making them happy, but if he truly cares about our country, he needs to start listening to all the people, not just a selected few.

Our president is beginning to lose the support of a portion of his base. He cannot afford this if he truly believes he is going to be in office for the next four to eight years. Eight years, according to him. No matter what the reasons may be for Clinton's loss, it's still important to remember that she still won the popular vote. We may never know if she would have won if Comey had not released those emails. We may never know if she would have won if we find evidence of Russian collusion in our election. It doesn't matter. The numbers are there. Trump won the electoral vote plain and simple. Why? Because he spoke to the people that Hillary missed. That's why.

In any case, if Trump loses even a small portion of his base and doesn't even try to expand, he will lose. I won't lose any sleep over this, mind you, but I'm guessing a whole lot of other people will. I loved President Obama, but I did not agree with every policy or piece of legislation he passed. I have a mind of my own and sometimes I may have disagreed. That doesn't mean I disliked Obama. I always he felt he was much smarter than me. I happen to like that in my president. I've heard it said that one of the main reasons that people didn't like him was that they found him condescending because he used big words and not common language. People felt he spoke down to them. I never felt that way. I found him smart, yes. Like I said. I want a smart president.

Apparently, the people that connect with Trump like him because he speaks to them on their level, or something to that effect. I refuse to believe that. The people in this country are not stupid. We do not need to be spoken to like idiots. Trump says what he feels even if it's rude, crude or obscene. Is that really what we want in an American President? I guess it is for some, but not for me. That's just my opinion, of course.

Remember, this book is being written as a political commentary so I am basically giving my opinion throughout. I do not intend to try to tell anybody how to think or to change anyone's mind.

So far, our president doesn't seem to use his Cabinet or the Congress for any of his legislation or policy making. He is his own man and doesn't seem to take advice from anyone. However, whenever something goes wrong he manages to find someone else to blame. It generally falls on his communications team, since they are the ones who delivered the message incorrectly which led to him being beaten up by the press.

It's all so crazy. He wants to be King, but he's ready to kill all the King's men if they don't live up to their full potential. That of course, changes every single hour. How do they keep up? Beats the heck out of me. He's already lost or fired a few of them. I'm sure more heads will roll. We'll just have to wait to see which ones and how many. I feel bad for them to tell you the truth. I guess we'll just have to wait to see how things shake out. In the meantime, let me continue to entertain you with my vast knowledge and incredible wisdom. I'm sure you're all dying to know what else I have in store. Stay tuned.

CHAPTER 10

The NATO Shove

We've all heard of dances like the Macarena, the Two-Step, the Slide and on and on; but how many of you have heard of the latest dance craze called "The NATO Shove"? I'm sure many of you saw it on the news. It was pretty amazing to watch. Maybe amazing is the wrong choice of words. Shocking might be more appropriate.

President Trump invented this little "dance". It was quite jaw dropping. The world watched as the President of the United States, after attending the G7 conference, managed to push his way through the crowd of NATO dignitaries and SHOVED one of them to the side so he could have his place in the front row of the picture. I am not talking about a polite nudge with an "excuse me". I am talking about a hard push to the side without any apology. He looked just like a schoolyard bully only giant sized. It would have been funny if it hadn't been so embarrassing for our country. Believe me, it was definitely embarrassing.

I take no pleasure in saying that this president has no idea of diplomacy. It doesn't make me feel good to say that I was right not to vote for him. When I say I wanted him to succeed; I am sincere. This country is in more danger from countries like North Korea and from terrorism than ever before. We need strong leadership. What we do not need is a leader who feels most comfortable behind his twitter account making remarks that are insulting mainly to those countries that are our allies.

He's playing a very dangerous game. He has a few good people in his cabinet that he should be listening to when it comes to both foreign and domestic affairs; but he simply refuses to listen. He feels he is the smartest of them all. No one man can be the smartest on all topics, no matter how smart they are. Trump needs to acknowledge this. Until he does, our country doesn't stand a chance. I wouldn't want to be the one to try to explain this to him. Remember, he IS the smartest guy in the room after all. Pay no attention to that IQ stuff.

That stuff doesn't mean anything. It's money that matters and Trump has lots of that.

This Page Intentionally Left Blank

CHAPTER 11

ISIS and Terrorism

So, what do you say when someone tells you the answer to terrorism is to go in and blow them all up? I've heard more than one person say this to me. My reaction? Which country do you plan to blow up first? This theory makes no sense. ISIS is a terrorist organization that is based on an ideology which they have managed to spread mainly through our youth all throughout the world.

There are terrorist cells in all parts of the world now. We know this because of the many attacks in Britain, France, Germany and other parts of the world. So, what do we do? Do we obliterate France? Do we bomb the Hell out of Germany? Do we nuke Britain? Come on! Let's get serious here. Sure, we know the major cells are in Syria, Libya, Afghanistan and places throughout the Middle East.

Even so, we still can't go in and just nuke these entire countries killing hundreds of thousands of innocents in an effort to kill thousands of terrorists. We are supposed to be humanitarians, not terrorists ourselves. There are many, many innocent men, women and children trying to escape the horrible conditions they are currently forced to live under in these countries. Most countries will no longer accept them as refugees as they are now perceived as threats. The irony here is just sad. These people are basically trapped.

To date, our president has taken measured action against terrorism for which I am grateful. When he bombed the airstrip in Syria; I was relieved he didn't go any further. He listened to his military advisors, thankfully.

Since that time however, he has repeatedly made several inappropriate and very insulting remarks toward our allies in their handling of terrorism. Rather than offering U.S. sympathy and support; he chooses to insult them. Where's the diplomacy? Will our allies be there for us when and if the time comes that we need them? These are all important questions that need to be asked. I fear they may not unless this president changes his tune very quickly. His learning curve is coming to a very quick end.

Getting back to the "bomb them all" theory; let's just say for the sake of argument that we did just that. Where exactly would you start? My suggestion would be Syria. Of course, many innocent people would die, but hey! That's just too bad, right? Better them than us. I guess that's the reasoning, huh? Then where? Remember now, ISIS has cells all over the world now. When do we stop? Do we just keep bombing every single country that has a terrorist attack? That's a little bit extreme, yes? I'm guessing even those of you who say, "bomb them all" wouldn't be in favor of bombing France, England or Germany? Or would you?

ISIS is an ideology. They are not a religion. They are not Muslims. They claim to be, but they are not true to Islam. If you have ever known a Muslim, you probably know them as kind and gentle and without a violent bone in their body. I once worked with a Muslim. This person once revealed to me that they were Muslim and had to ask me not to share that information with anyone for fear that they would not be accepted as a friend anymore. To this day, I have not told a soul and it still breaks my heart that this kind person has to keep their religion a secret. What a shame. Nobody in this country should ever have to hide their religion. Nobody in this country should be ashamed of the color of their skin. Nobody in this country should be afraid to speak. This is America!

The only way to kill ISIS is to somehow to kill the ideology. How? Well, my best guess is to try to reach the same young people that ISIS is reaching and do it through the same channels, the internet. If we use the same technology they use, we just might have a chance. Or, I may be full of it. Sure, we still need to knock out their headquarters; but we don't need to take out a bunch of innocent lives along with them. The use of modern technology along with military action should be able to accomplish a great deal. It won't stop it; but it will slow it down.

CHAPTER 12

Conflicts of Interest- Gee, Ya Think?

Do you think there are any conflicts of interest in this White House or are you perfectly comfortable with things the way they are? We are certainly in a unique situation. Never have we had a business mogul in the White House. This is new territory. There are bound to be monetary conflicts previously never encountered.

Is this a problem? Possibly. Probably in my opinion. When Mr. Trump was campaigning, he said he would separate himself and his family from the family business in order to avoid any sense of impropriety. He no sooner got elected and he did a complete turnaround. Suddenly, he said it wasn't necessary for him to get rid of his business. Then, he said he would be willing to give it to his sons, but he wouldn't be involved. So, just exactly how is this supposed to work?

Are we just supposed to believe that if Trump or even Ivanka or Jared (who now have access to classified information as well) should come across some highly valuable information that could potentially make the Trump Corporation a ton of money, will just stay quiet about it and not "accidently" say something to Eric or Don Jr. at the dinner table someday? Sorry, I'm not that trusting.

We also have a little thing called nepotism. You may be familiar with the term. The White House is beginning to look more like a family business than a government. For the life of me, I am still trying to figure out why both Jared Kushner and Ivanka Trump have offices in the West Wing as well as access to classified information. I mean really? Access to the most important information our country has is now being given to two people who have absolutely no government background whatsoever.

I'm sure they are both very intelligent people. Don't get me wrong, but there are plenty of smart people in this country that have no right to classified government information, nor should they. The fact that these two are still closely tied to the Trump Organization should keep them as far away from this type of information as possible. Instead, they are right in the middle of it. Like I said, nepotism. Then of course, we have all the Russian ties with both the Trump and Kushner family businesses. How this affects our government is yet to be determined and that is partially why we are having these hearings.

Of course, we are probably hoping to get a lot more out of these hearings than we probably will, but I'm sure we will get answers to a few of our questions, at least. For instance, why is Trump so darned afraid to show us his tax returns? Every other president has shown theirs. Why not Trump? Please don't tell me it's because he's being audited. The IRS has already indicated that his returns CAN be released. So, no excuse there.

Sorry Trump! Another lie. There are some 15 years or so of returns that he is having audited according to him. That's why he says it's taking so long. Think about that for a minute. Do you really believe for one minute that they finish them all at once? Of course not! Let's get with the program. He's hiding something and he needs time to find a way to cover it up before he can show them. By the time we see them, they'll probably all be on a 1040A. He's slick! I think what bothers me more than anything is the fact that the "true blue"

Trump supporters just plain don't care. That really upsets the heck out of me. Why the heck not? You all said you wanted a smart businessman to run our country. Why on God's green earth wouldn't you be interested to see his tax returns? Wouldn't you think they'd want to know how much money he has or how much he pays in taxes? Wouldn't you think they'd at the very least, want to make sure that everything he does with his finances are above board? After all, you did just vote to make him our President. I should think you'd want him to at least clear his name. No? Oh, okay. Next!

CHAPTER 13

The First Family

Should we be leaving the first family alone or are they fair game? What are your thoughts on this subject? I'll tell you mine. Try to contain yourselves. I know you're just biting at the bit.

As far the little ones go, it's completely hands off. We admire them and say how cute they are and that's about it. In this White House, Baron is hands off. He is a 10 or 11-year-old little boy who needs to be shielded as much as possible. From what I have seen of Melania, she appears to be a very protective mom. Good for her! I'll admit it bothers the heck out of me that I pay my tax dollars to help support her and her son live in New York rather than in the White House; but I understand her need to stay in New York with Baron until he gets out of school.

I just hope he gets out soon, because it's costing the American taxpayer a fortune keeping them in New York. From the look of it, Mr. and Mrs. Trump did not have all their ducks in a row when he decided to run for President of the United States. I don't think Melania looks at all happy to be First Lady. I think she's far more content being a mother. I have a funny feeling she wasn't really given much of a choice.

As for the other children. In my opinion at least, they have been a large part of the Trump campaign and two of them are now in even working alongside of him. These are adults who have chosen to put themselves in the limelight. They are not trying to shy away. If they are taking any heat, maybe it's ok. They are not young children and can certainly handle themselves.

The youngest daughter Tiffany seems chill. I don't think she enjoys the limelight all that much, but I do think she loves her dad and will support him when he asks. Most Trump fans seem to feel that the Trump children are models of perfection. I do not. I do however, like Tiffany. She seems very down to earth.

I do think Ivanka tries very hard to connect with young middle-class mothers, but generally misses the mark. It's very hard for her to relate on the same level with the average mother of two or three children with a husband and a total household income of say $70,000.

Compare that to the millionaire status of Ivanka, it's just not the same trying to squeeze out that weekly daycare check. I think Ivanka believes she understands, but I doubt that she really does. She was born rich, raised rich and married rich. She has never known anything different. So, is it even fair that we ask her to? She does seem to have a certain sweetness about her. I will give her that.

As for the two boys Don Jr. and Eric, I am less certain. They both seem to have a certain arrogance about them that I just don't like. They seem like the sort of college frat boys that would probably haze someone to the brink of death, just to watch them squirm. Eric concerns me the most with some of his tweets, but I will leave it at that. My feelings are mainly my gut reactions, that's all.

As for our new First Lady Melania Trump, she is no doubt a beautiful woman. Other than that, it's hard to comment, isn't it? The only time I see her is when she shows up for a dignitary function or some fancy dinner.

Other than that, I have not seen her give any speeches since the Inauguration, nor has she done any work to stop bullying that I am aware of. After all, if she had, maybe her hubby wouldn't be doing the NATO Shove. (That was just supposed to be a little funny there, get it?) Sometimes I'm just not all that funny. That's why I need to spell it out when I tell you I just told a joke. I need to make you recognize it so you don't take offense to it.

Aren't you excited to see what other funnies lie in wait. Well, just read on. I'll try not to disappoint.

CHAPTER 14

James Comey

This week James Comey is supposed to testify before the special prosecutor. Everyone is expecting some huge revelation. While that would certainly be wonderful, I am not so hopeful. Call it the cynic in me. From what I understand, the hearing is going to be done in an open format and shown on Public Television.

Whose stupid idea was that? Sure, I'm as anxious to hear what he has to say as everybody else, but let's face it; he's not about to say anything that could compromise national security in a public forum. He's a man of honor by all accounts and he isn't going to do or say anything that was said in a private setting with the president in front of a bunch of cameras. That's just my feeling. He will answer questions that do not relate to our nation's security perhaps, but I doubt seriously if he will go any further.

We will soon find out as tomorrow the hearing begins. This chapter will continue after tomorrow. Time for this little old woman to take a serious break. See ya on the other side.

Well, I'm on the other side of the Comey hearing and it turns out that I was wrong. There, I said it! I WAS WRONG! It has been known to happen more than once. How many times is between me and God. Sorry, not gonna tell. Besides, I don't think I can remember how to count that high anymore.

All that aside, I was very pleasantly surprised to see that Comey was very open with the Senators and answered almost all their questions, except for the ones that could only be answered in a classified setting. I'm sure you're all just dying to know my opinion of the hearing. Well, here it is. Confused. For someone so obviously brilliant as myself, you'd certainly think I'd have a better answer than that, wouldn't you? Too bad, that's all I've got.

In case you're wondering why I say that, let me explain. I try to listen to both sides and get both perspectives before I decide on where I stand on any particular issue. The Comey case is a very complicated one and both sides have made some very valid points.

If you listen to the Democrats, they are still mad at Comey for releasing those emails, but they have very high expectations and are hoping that Comey is going to be the key to finally bringing Trump down.

If you listen to the Trump supporters, Comey has just exonerated Trump from all collusion and has now branded himself a "leaker". First, let's not forget, this hearing was not about collusion or Russia. This hearing was strictly about obstruction of justice. The President has not been exonerated of anything just yet. Nothing has yet been decided. These hearings are not over. This is going to take a while.

For me? I say the truth lies somewhere in the middle. The real story remains to be told and probably won't be heard until a long way down the road. I believe that some of the classified information probably told a much larger portion of the story. Do the American people deserve to know that story? Not if it could endanger our National Security they don't. I know, I'm kind of funny like that. I feel strongly that the people's right to know ends when our nation's security is at risk.

I do have an opinion however. When I first saw Comey walk into the room and take a seat; I felt sorry for the man. Yes, I am angry about the emails too, but let's face it; who hasn't screwed up big time at least a few times in their life? I know I have. As he sat there with that stoic look on his face with all those cameras shooting picture after picture after picture, my Lord! How could you not at least have a tiny bit of sympathy for that man. I'm sure a great deal of you disagree with me and that is certainly your right. I guess I'm just a bit of a softee. All I can say is that I wouldn't have wanted to be him at that moment, that's for darned sure.

Then came the orators. That's what I call them anyway. Boy, those guys sure do like to hear themselves talk. I should have been a Senator. I LOVE to talk. If I'd been a Senator, maybe I wouldn't be in the predicament I'm in now. I'd sure as heck have better healthcare and a nice pension. I digress.

Once they finished talking, they gave Mr. Comey an opportunity to address the crowd. He gave what I thought was a very heartfelt opening speech. He thanked the country, the FBI and his former co-workers for the opportunity to serve. He apologized to his co-workers for not having had the chance to say good-bye to each of them. How could he? He was fired while he was out of town as his desk was cleaned out for him. Tacky! I thought he was very gracious and almost on the verge of tears. Maybe I'm wrong. Again, it happens a lot.

We found out quite a few things during the testimony. Some of it I found extremely relevant, some not so much. I will just touch on a few of the ones I found most interesting to me. I'm sure you will all have your own.

When asked about the time he met with the President a day after Michael Flynn had been fired, Mr. Comey testified that the President asked Attorney General Sessions and his son-in-law Jared Kushner to both leave the room so he could speak to

Mr. Comey in private. Once he had Mr. Comey alone, he basically asked him to "let it go" when referring to the Flynn investigation stating, "he's a good guy". Comey's reply? "He's a good guy." I have a problem with that reply. Comey said he was stunned. I'm sure in hindsight he wishes he had said something different, but he didn't. He said it.

This probably gave Trump the wrong impression. Remember, Trump is a narcissist. He thinks the world rises and sets on him and everyone is at his beckoned call, even the FBI. They are basically the hired help.

While I have a problem with Comey's answer, I have an even bigger problem with the fact that Sessions left the room, leaving the FBI Director alone with the President. I'm going to pretend to agree that Paul Ryan is correct in stating that President Trump simply doesn't understand correct protocol because he's never been in government before. Let's just say that's true. What about Sessions? He knows, right? Why didn't he step in? He was Comey's superior. He should have stepped in and told Trump right then and there that he needed to be in the room for any conversation with the FBI director. Instead, he just walked out.

Another big conversation was at the dinner on February 14th, Valentine's Day of all days. Comey had to break a date with his wife in order to have dinner with the President of the United States. Of course, you don't exactly tell the President "sorry, I already have a date, sir". He was assuming there would be other people at this dinner. To his surprise, it was just him and the President. The President decided to take this opportunity to ask Mr. Comey if he intended to keep his job. He then advised him that he required complete loyalty and asked Comey if he would be willing to give him that. Comey offered the President his complete honesty.

The President again asked for his loyalty and again Comey offered honesty to which the President offered to accept Honest Loyalty to which Comey agreed. Really? Once Comey got back to his vehicle he decided to make extensive notes of his meeting with the President, as his feeling was that he might someday need to recall his conversations word for word. since he was afraid that the President might lie about something or he may need to recall his conversations at a later date given the awkward nature of the conversation. As it happens, this is probably the smartest move Comey made.

When Comey heard on television that he had been terminated as FBI Director and the President began tweeting that the FBI was in terrible disarray; it then became apparent to Mr. Comey that the only way to reach the truth was to get his notes to the Press. Since the press was surrounding his home; he decided to ask a close friend of his to take his private notes to the New York Times.

His hope was that these notes would prompt the hiring of a Special Prosecutor which it did. It was pretty clever when you think about it. It was obvious that most people wanted a Special Prosecutor, but since Congress has a Republican majority, they were dragging their feet. Oh sure, there are several Republicans (mostly Senators) that were pushing for the Special Prosecutor, but the majority were perfectly satisfied that they could handle things "in house" so to speak. To me, this would be like asking members of your extended family to preside over your murder trial. No bias there, right?

I think the one thing that probably troubled me the very most throughout the entire hearing wasn't anything to do with any criminal activity, but simply our own national security. When Comey was asked if the President ever asked Russia's interference or how they may be involved in our elections, Comey replied that the President never asked. Now you may not think this is a big deal or maybe you do, but to me this is pretty huge. Our nation's security is at risk from Russia and our President isn't even concerned enough to ask about it. This should have been one of the top things on his list. His cavalier attitude toward Russia is just too strange. It makes me very uncomfortable.

Maybe he's directly involved and maybe not, but I think he knows more than he's saying. Either way, as things stand right now, neither Comey nor President Trump look too good. Let's face it, we are all biased in the way we interpret the facts. I may see them one way and you may see them another way. It's called human nature. It's only natural. If you're a Democrat, you are probably going to believe that Comey's testimony was damning. If you are a Trump supporter, you are probably going to believe his testimony exonerated the President of all charges. Like I said, human nature.

It's one man's word against another. Comey says Trump lied. Trump says Comey lied. So, who do you believe? Comey was under oath. Trump has offered to testify under oath. Let's face it though. When a person testifies under oath, it isn't like they take a magic pill that suddenly forces them to tell the truth. Just because they put their hand on a bible, doesn't necessarily mean they are incapable of telling a lie.

Take President Trump. He lies as easily as he breathes. Sometimes I think he even believes his own lies. Heck, at his age he may even remember things incorrectly for all we know. I know I do. So, if he gets on the stand and swears under oath that something is true and we later find truth that it isn't; how do we prove his intent was to lie? Maybe he thought he was telling the truth. That's a little unnerving, isn't it? Ahhhh, the twists and turns. Don't you love it? This is just a small taste of what it's like being inside my head. Scary huh?

I must admit that I would love to be a little mouse in the corner of the classified hearings. Wouldn't you? I don't think I have any right to know that information, but I'd love to hear it anyway. I'm just so darned curious to know what he had to say. Not just him, the rest of them as well. I know that Sessions is supposed to testify next week and if I'm correct, so is Flynn. I'd love to hear what those two have to say. The last I heard Sessions will be deposed in a closed session. I think they should keep it that way, no matter how curious I may be. I'm not sure about

Flynn. I think his hearings are scheduled to be both public and closed. Frankly, I don't think I'd believe a word he says, even though he's been granted immunity. We'll just have to see what he says I guess. Maybe he'll tell the truth and maybe he won't.

The President has been playing games about the tapes. He loves to tease the press. It's all just a great big reality show to him. None of this is real to him. It may not concern some of you, but it sure concerns the heck out of me. In response to Comey's testimony, Trump said "No collusion, no corruption, he's a leaker". Well, as I stated earlier, the hearing wasn't to address the Russian collusion, merely the obstruction of justice.

So again, he has missed the point. As far as being a leaker is concerned, just for a moment let's try to put ourselves in Comey's position. First, to the Republicans' point, the notes were taken while he was still the Director of the FBI. I understand their concern on that point. However, the notes themselves were not of a classified nature and at the time of their release to the press he was a private citizen. Does this make it ok?

Under normal circumstances, I would probably have to say "no". This case is unusual however. Like I said, let's put ourselves in Comey's shoes. He didn't feel he could safely go to the Attorney General (Sessions) at the time because Sessions himself was probably already being investigated for Russian collusion and Comey knew there was a direct conflict of interest there considering how close Sessions was to the President. Since the President still hadn't filled most of the positions in the Department of Justice (DOJ), there was nobody else for him to consult with, so he chose to take notes or memos, if you will, and once he was fired released them to the press with the hope that these memos would prompt an investigation by a special investigator. It did. Could his plan have backfired? Sure it could; but it didn't, did it? I honestly think Comey felt like he was just trapped between a rock and a hard place. I think he did something extreme to get himself out of an extreme situation. That is just the way I see it. I'm sure many of you see it differently, which is certainly your prerogative.

So, let's get back to those so-called tapes. I wonder how many of you believe that there are any tapes at all? Me? I truly do not. If there ever were; they have already been destroyed. Yes,

I know. I sound like a nut job. I even admit to it. I'll bet I'm not alone though. Think about it. Is it really that outrageous that people would doubt the existence of such tapes? This President has made outrageous claims before that never came to fruition.

He first told us that he was going to show us his tax returns when President Obama showed us his birth certificate and that didn't happen. Then he said he would show them after he was elected; that didn't happen. Then he said he couldn't release them until they were done being audited. The IRS has disputed that, so he again lied there. Then he finally said he just plain isn't going to show them because AMERICA doesn't care. YES, WE DO! At least most us do. Who is he talking about? His base? His base is not the majority; and even some of his base would like to see his taxes. This guy doesn't get it. Those returns could put a lot of people's minds to rest. If he truly doesn't have anything to hide; just show them. It's just that simple.

He has also made claims to have absolute proof that Obama wiretapped Trump Tower. Again, another lie. After he tweeted this out, he basically ordered his communications team to go out and FIND the truth so he didn't look bad to the press.

He makes statements like this with no proof and then wonders why the press jumps on him. He brings trouble onto himself and then blames the people around him. He has never shown any accountability for his own actions. The only time he apologized was for the bus incident and that was strictly because he knew his nomination was at risk if he didn't own up to it. Plain and simple.

So, why should we believe this time is any different? If Trump truly had any dirt on Comey he would have already released it. My guess is there were never any tapes to be had. If there were, they did not look good for the President or he would have already produced them. Now, if he's truly as honorable and law abiding as many of his supporters think he is; he has them and he will produce them, flattering or not.

Only time will tell. Either way, Bob Mueller is done playing games and has demanded the tapes by June 23rd. Why that date? I don't have any idea. Why give him that much time to edit or destroy? I would have just demanded that he produce them within 48 hours. I can be awfully mean sometimes. Supposedly, the President has now agreed to tell us whether they even "exist" sometime within the next week or so. He's a generous soul, isn't he? Again, with the games. He's such a fun guy. I think I'm crackin' up.

CHAPTER 15

Sessions in Session

What is your impression of Jeff Sessions? At first, I thought he just seemed like a sweet little Southern gentleman who was probably a little behind the times and possibly somewhat racist. I didn't really like him that much, but I didn't dislike him either. I'm still not sure what to make of him to be honest. He looks so darned innocent. He could be anybody's little old grandpa, right? Well, maybe not.

I choose to cut him a little slack. Not because I like the guy, but rather because of his age and the fact that he was brought up in the South. Perhaps I'm a little guilty of stereotyping here, but back in the 50's and 60's, the South was very racist. It wasn't exactly uncommon for children of that time to be brought up in that culture. When you are brought up a certain way, right or wrong, sometimes it's hard to shake those old traditions. I think it's possible that is where Sessions fits in. Like him or don't, at least try to understand him.

I have been living with my beautiful daughter and granddaughter here in Texas for the past year and half or more due to illness. I am better now and looking forward to moving back to Arizona to live on my own. I have observed several behaviors while living in Texas that I feel are worth mentioning. Although I have not lived here that long, it has made an impression on me; some good, some bad. The first thing you notice is that people down South have wonderful manners. Everything is "yes, ma'am or no, ma'am". My children were always brought up with very good manners, but I find that good manners are very hard to find generally.

In the South, people are very well-mannered. However, these good manners do not always translate into good deeds or kindness. I find the South to be very narrow-minded. You would think the Bible Belt would be more accepting, but they are not. They are far more racist and do not believe in gay rights at all. I happen to believe very strongly that it is not my right to judge.

Only God holds the right to judge a person's sexuality. Besides, I refuse to believe that anyone would CHOOSE to be gay. God created that person the way they are. It's a hard life for a person to be gay in a world where they are ridiculed and even tortured or killed. Why on earth would someone choose that for themselves? The same is true for any member of the LGBT community. I mean come on! Have some compassion. Where's that so-called Christianity? Like I said, manners do not equal kindness or understanding. I will say that Texas is certainly a beautiful state and for the most part, the people here are very nice.

On a more serious note, let's discuss the Russian investigation. This is a whole different ball of wax. Sessions took some tough questions. I'm not quite sure what to make of his answers. A lot of his answers were "I do not recall" or my favorite and the one that made no sense at all was something to the effect "I can't answer in case the

President decides to invoke his right to Executive Privilege". He wasn't invoking it himself; as he acknowledged he could not do that, but he wouldn't answer just in case the President wanted to, if deposed. HUH? This is just one of the many reasons people get so frustrated with our government officials. In my opinion, they should not have even held this hearing in a public setting. I know I've said this before, but just because the American people may have a RIGHT to know something, doesn't mean we SHOULD. If the hearing had been held in a classified setting, we may have learned more. We will never know, as Sessions doesn't seem to have a very good memory. Then again, neither did Comey.

It pretty much depends on who you choose to believe, doesn't it? My guess is, if you are a Republican, you are probably going to be more inclined to believe Sessions. If you are a Democrat, you will probably be more inclined to believe Comey. Pick one! In my extremely valued opinion, both these men present with problems. They both seem to have gaps in their memories.

Now, if you were asked a series of questions with a total of possibly up to 8 or 9 different dates, do you think you could remember vivid details? I can honestly answer that question with an unequivocal "no". I just got back from Arizona a few weeks ago and I can't even remember which dates I was gone. I'd have to check my emails. Perhaps that's why I tend not to judge either one of these men too harshly when it comes to their memories.

Where I have a larger problem is when they simply refuse to answer due to some privacy issue. I felt that when Comey cited the need to answer under closed session; he was sincere. I took him more seriously. While Sessions seemed convincingly angered and insulted by the accusations being brought against him; his excuses for not answering many of the questions posed to him were simply not feasible and unbelievable. Whether Comey or Sessions is telling the truth will remain to be seen.

Hopefully, Robert Mueller will be able to get to the bottom of it all. Only time will tell. Let's just hope President Trump doesn't decide to fire Mueller like he did Comey. The rumor mill is having a field day with that story. I won't presume to speak for you guys, but I'm tired of the press constantly reporting rumors. If they are rumors; leave it alone until you know for a fact that the story is true. That's just my personal opinion. I am a strong believer in the First Amendment and the Freedom of the Press. That doesn't mean I can't be frustrated at the same time when they report things before all the facts are in. Cable News is the worst. Yes, I am a guilty viewer of Cable News. I enjoy being kept in the loop. I also recognize when I'm being fed a bunch of innuendo and supposition rather than actual news supported by facts.

Many people who watch do not. This is disturbing. Part of the reason so many people in this country are so angry is simply because of something they have heard either on Cable News or read on Facebook or Twitter. That's no way to get real news. My advice?

You can watch Cable News, but only if you also watch an hour or so of "regular nightly news" like ABC, CBS or NBC. At least then, you're more apt to get a non-biased view of the news. Cable is almost always biased either to the left or to the right. If I'm honest, I will tell you that I enjoy watching CNN. Why you ask? While they are more liberal than conservative, they always have a panel of journalists and other professionals that also give the conservative viewpoint.

While I may not always agree, I at least feel that I am getting a more rounded and full account of the story. From there, I can more easily make up my mind as to where the truth really lies. It's generally somewhere in the middle. While it's certainly easier to listen only to people who agree with me, Lord knows my ulcers prefer it; I prefer to hear the facts rather than conjecture and opinion. I do not listen to Fox or even MSNBC. Both are too extreme for my taste. I am more of a moderate and I am not ashamed to say so. I think most of us are, but probably aren't being heard. The extremists are the loudest and get the most press. If you only want to listen to people who agree with you, then by all means, choose your favorite Cable channel and go for it. I'll pass, thank you. I just want the truth. Yes, I can handle the truth! At least, I think so.

CHAPTER 16

A House Divided

I'm quite sure I am not alone in my thinking. Our government needs an entire overhaul. Is it the Republicans' fault or the Democrats'? Does it even matter? What matters is that both parties are acting like idiots right now and they don't seem to be placing the country's interests before the interests of their own, individual party. This is a huge problem for us as Americans.

Why? Both parties have been guilty of trying to pass legislation that has some sort of crazy addendum attached to it that has nothing to do with the actual bill itself. The other party of course rejects it. I will try to give you a fake example.

Let's say for instance that the Democrats wanted to pass some sort of bill that had to do with requiring safety belts on school buses. Let's say that the Republicans would be apt to approve it. Then just for grins, the Democrats decide to sneak a little addendum to the bill that also allows more restrictions on gun sales. Guess what happens? Of course, the Republicans say "no" to the bill, right? So, then the Democrats start screaming that those terrible Republicans don't care about our children enough to vote for seat belts in school buses, making it seem like the Republicans are heartless and it was all about the seat belts, not because of the addendum that was attached at the very end.

To be clear, both parties do this all the time. I'm not just picking on the Democrats. I'm just trying to level the playing field a little and it seemed like a good example. Remember, this is not a real scenario. I was just trying to make a point.

Congress is refusing to work together right now. It hasn't been working for quite a while. It started during the Bush administration and really took a bad turn during the Obama administration. It has not improved. If anything, it's even worse. If I had any hope at all for Trump, it was that he might be able to reunite the two parties, since the division was so obvious during the Obama years. It was heartbreaking to watch. We had a president who was willing to work with both parties, but they simply refused to work with him in kind. At first, it was just the Republicans. After it became apparent that he was having trouble getting things done fast enough for the public, he began to lose the approval of many Americans. Once that happened, he even started losing the approval of many of his own Democrats in Congress.

Why? Because they didn't want to back a President with low ratings in case their constituents decided not to vote for them strictly because of their allegiance to the President. It wasn't until President Obama made the announcement that the military had confirmed that Osama Bin Laden had been located and killed that his ratings finally began to turn around and he started to gain more respect. Of course, by that time the damage had already been done and the voters spoke. We now have an all Republican majority in both houses of our Congress. I have nothing against the Republicans, but I do have a problem when both houses are controlled by one party. It means that the other party no longer matters. In many ways, you would think it would make our government work better, since you would imagine that the gridlock would no longer exist.

Unfortunately, it hasn't happened that way. Why? Sadly, neither side of the aisle happened to like President Obama. I don't know why exactly. I've heard he was arrogant and spoke down to people. People just didn't connect with him. While it's true that he was very articulate, I never felt that way; but then I happen to want a President who is smarter than me. Call me crazy. You wouldn't be the first.

When Trump came into office, we had the same problem. Neither side liked him either for the most part, although I do see the Republicans trying their level best to make excuses for him at every turn. A few will step forward and try to show their dissatisfaction, but if you listen to their words, then watch what they actually "do", you will notice they still fall in line with the "Party". Very few will stray too far from the nest, but no legislation has yet to be passed either. In that respect at least, they are making their voices heard. Is this helping the American people? It's hard to say.

No "bad" legislation is going through, but no "good" legislation is going through either. Congress is deadlocked. The Democrats are just saying "no" to everything and the Republicans can't seem to come up with any new ideas that they can all agree on either, so even they can't get a majority vote on any big legislation. Meanwhile, the President is just going crazy with his executive orders unraveling every bill that Obama managed to pass during his term. Sure, he's managed to get several bills passed that are minor like naming Parks or getting rid of regulations on bills that Obama passed.

Most of his legislation was passed through Executive Order, the rest was a piece of cake as the Republicans own both houses in Congress and these are not big pieces of legislation. We still need healthcare and tax reform. These are bills that are still being debated. It is not an easy task; yet our President said he thought it would be "so easy". When he realized the enormity of the task at hand, his response? "Nobody knew this would be so hard". Yes, they did! Where has he been the last decade? In a sand trap on the golf course or in the boardroom? Either way, this is not the best use of our Congress, is it? Every time I hear that Congress is out of session; it makes me cringe.

They barely get anything done even when they're "in session". Yet, they seem to need a lot of "breaks" from all their hard work. I used to get 2 weeks, then later 3 weeks of vacation with 5 sick days. Anything over that I didn't get paid for. I think that same rule should apply to our Congress. Maybe they'd try harder. There isn't one person I have spoken to who doesn't agree that we need shorter Congressional terms. The tricky part is just exactly how we go about getting something like this done. After all, are you going to write to your

Congressmen and ask them if they'd be willing to sign legislation shortening their terms? I'm sure they'd jump at the chance, right? This is one of platforms that President Trump ran on. He could really help us out here if he wanted to. Of course, even if he did sign an executive order; I believe (and I could be mistaken) a 2/3 vote by Congress could overrule him. It would still be a good start. I simply believe that no Congressman should be allowed to serve more than two terms. After all, if that's all the President can serve, why do we allow our Congressmen to serve term after term after term.

Of course, as voters, we also have a responsibility. If your state Senator or Representative has already served for two terms; just don't keep voting for them. The problem with most voters is that they do not educate themselves on the candidates that run for these state positions. I, myself have been guilty of this on many occasions. I just vote for the person whose name I am most familiar with. I'm sure that many of you have done the same thing. The reason so many of our Senators and Representatives are so darned old is because they've been in that same office for so long. They have far more financial backing that any newcomer will have and their name recognition alone generally continues to get them reelected.

Perhaps President Trump will keep this campaign promise. It would sure be a great start. I'm guessing the people would be outraged if their state's Senators and Representatives voted against Trump to reverse that executive order, knowing how many people want this. Their chances of getting re-elected would be at great risk. Are you listening Congress? Ok, Yikes! I woke today to some rather shocking and distressing news. Sure, I'm frustrated as heck with Congress and the gridlock. Let me be perfectly clear about something however. In no way, shape or form have I EVER condoned violence as a resolution to a problem of any nature. Certainly not when it involves our government.

Today another nutcase with a gun decided to take matters into his own hands and take several shots at many of our Republicans while they were practicing for a charity baseball game. Apparently, once a year, both Republicans and Democrats come together and have a bipartisan baseball game for charity. They were trying to do something GOOD for our country. This is one of the few times when they actually put their politics aside and just do something good for charity. This shooter then took this opportunity of all times, to shoot them down like ducks in a pond. I don't care what your political affiliation is; this is just plain wrong. Shooting people in no way is the answer to anything. It resolved nothing. Luckily it appears that all will survive, but one is severely injured and will have to undergo several surgeries. This is just plain crazy. Yes, I am a Democrat, but I do not believe in shooting our Republican Congressmen. This goes against my sense of humanity and my Christian beliefs.

The only thing this gunman achieved was getting himself killed. Maybe that was his plan all along. How did that help? Did that do anything other than to cause a great deal of pain to others? What about his own family?

Did he stop to think of them? It certainly didn't do anything to shorten Congressional terms and more than likely it still won't stop the rhetoric from either side for more than maybe a month when all of this will be forgotten.

Remember how severely people were affected by the tragedy of 9/11? I thought for sure our country would come together and unite after such a tragedy. Oh sure, we did for about 5 months. Every time I'm in an airport and I hear somebody complain about having to take their stupid shoes off; I just want to slug them and scream, "don't you remember 9/11?". We seem to have very short memories. We live very protected lives here in America and we are quite spoiled. If you ever have the opportunity to visit a country like Africa, for instance, maybe you'd appreciate it more. I have not, but I know people who have; and the stories I've heard are heartbreaking.

Unfortunately, I don't see an end to this type of anger any time soon. Sadly, people are just out of control when it comes to controlling their anger. There is basically no such thing as self-control anymore. People are "losing it". I'm no psychologist so I have no answer for this dilemma.

While I may agree with the shooter's beliefs on some level, I am strongly against his methods. We need Congressional reform before people will stop being so darned angry. No amount of shooting or killing will help.

Our country has never been more divided. At least, not that my memory serves me. I just hope that somehow, we can find a way to come together without having to go through another 9/11 to get us there. It shouldn't take a tragedy to wake us up.

My advice to Congress? Grow up and play nice! America is tired of your games. There's plenty of room in the sandbox for all you to play.

This Page Intentionally Left Blank

CHAPTER 17

Racism – Alive and Well

I wasn't quite sure if I should touch on this subject in my book or not, but I believe it's important so I'm going to take the leap. Members of my own family and I have very different opinions on this subject. Not because they are racist, quite the opposite. In fact, if you were to ask them, they would tell you absolutely not, I'm quite sure.

However, every time there is another white cop on black shooting, they immediately jump to the defense of the cop; even before all the evidence is in; not because they don't like blacks, but because they have such enormous respect for the police. The Trayvon Martin case is the best example I can offer. Once I heard the original 9-1-1 tape of the dispatcher ordering Mr. Zimmerman to stay in his car and return home to let the police handle it; I knew at that time there was more to this story. I was told that Trayvon had either a Facebook, Twitter or Instagram account expressing his deep hatred of the police, so he was no angel and therefore, George Zimmerman was within his right to be following him with his gun that night as Trayvon was obviously up to no good.

While I do not agree that a boy that age should not have been out at that time of the night; I do not know the circumstances of why he was out. In any case, he was not doing anything wrong. He was merely buying Skittles and a can of soda. Whether or not he looked suspicious to George Zimmerman is completely beside the point here. Once Zimmerman was told to stay in his vehicle, he crossed the line.

The fact that he chose to follow a young man knowing full well that he was armed with a gun, just made him that much more culpable. He did not know anything about Trayvon Martin's twitter account (or whatever). He did not know him personally. He had no idea what kind of kid he was. All he knew was that he was a black kid wearing a hoodie.

That alone made him suspicious in Zimmerman's eyes. If you had a chance to listen to the entire 9-1-1 tape, you'll know what I mean. Any boy that age who is walking alone at night gand is being followed by a vehicle would obviously be scared; especially when the person inside the vehicle decides to get out of his vehicle and approach the boy. It shouldn't be at all surprising that Trayvon decided to fight Zimmerman off. We'll never know if Trayvon spotted Zimmerman's gun or not, so he used his only weapon; his fists. It was an entirely unfair fight. An advantage Zimmerman knew he had and could have avoided if he had just decided to stay in his car as he was told.

There was not one black person on that jury. Does that seem fair to you? It surely doesn't to me, but maybe I'm the one who's prejudiced, ha? Please don't misunderstand me. I am completely sympathetic to the plight of the police and the difficulty of the task at hand. I would hate to have to make some of the choices they make. I truly don't know how they do it. What I do know, is that it takes a very special type of person to be an officer. You must have a certain temperament. You can't be a hothead and you can't profile based on the color of a person's skin.

That can't always be easy. I have never had a run-in with any police officer. I never intend to. I have far too much respect for what they do. I am not taking sides. I am merely pointing out that there are certain officers that should not be on the job. The vast majority of officers are awesome. It only takes a few to make the rest look bad. We need to make sure that doesn't happen.

If it was just this one case, I'd leave it alone. Sadly, it has been case after case after case. Tonight, I heard that the jury failed to find the officer who shot and killed the young black man who worked at a school so closely with children while he was in a car simply trying to find his I.D. while his girlfriend's 4-year-old child sat in the backseat, guilty.

According to the jury, the officer simply overreacted after learning that the man had a gun; information that the man voluntarily offered. If he had intended to use his gun, do you really think he'd tell the officer "Dude, I've got a gun!". Good gravy! Use your head. If a police officer can't keep his cool, he has no business being an officer, does he? He should have at the very least been charged with manslaughter. I know this is a highly sensitive subject which is why I really struggled as to whether or not to put it in my book.

I feel very strongly about racism and think it's a discussion worth having, no matter how difficult it may be. Blacks are not the only ones who suffer from discrimination, so do people of Mexican descent as well as many other cultures. I have been guilty of prejudice myself. I think to try to deny that we are free of any type of prejudice is just lying to ourselves. We are all guilty on some level. Some are just more than others.

When I try to explain to my children or grandchildren about prejudice back in the 60's, sometimes I feel like it goes in one ear and out the other. After all, they've HEARD about Martin Luther King and seen pictures of him on TV, but they don't REMEMBER him. I do. I vividly remember stories of Jane Pittman drinking from the water fountain for the first time. I was only 6, but I still have vague memories of Rosa Parks when she refused to give her seat on the bus to a white person. That was a huge deal back then. Never had a black woman ever been so defiant to a white person prior to that time. To think that a black woman who was sitting in the black section of the bus was told to give up her seat to a white male is simply atrocious to me. Yet, it happened. This brave woman simply refused. She'd had enough. You would not believe the uproar. She was hailed by some and hated by many. Martin Luther King, Rosa Parks and Jane Pittman are just a few of many that helped changed black history.

When I hear someone young say "yeah, but that was then"; this is now. Things are different and the black people have it much better now, I just want to shake them. Why do you think the new generation is so angry if everything is so great? They are still being discriminated against. Just look at all these shootings, for Pete's sake. If that doesn't tell you anything, I don't know what will. I know that many of you think these shootings are all justified and I am sure that some of them are, but I'm sure that not ALL of them are. Think about the number of these shootings and then look at how many times the officers have been acquitted. Almost always. Coincidence? I don't think so.

For me, racism is very real as I lived through the riots and the marches. For my children and grandchildren, while they understand that those things happened; they are just stories from the "old days". They don't matter quite as much because today's generation didn't have to go through that. I think that's the difference and that's why racism hits me harder than it does them. They are not racists. They just don't always recognize it when they see it. I hope that makes sense.

Let's take the case of the young man I was speaking about earlier with the child in the back seat. His name was Philando Castile. His jury was comprised of 7 men and 5 women, including only 2 blacks. Apparently, the jury was deadlocked on Wednesday 10 in favor of acquittal and 2 against. According to one of the jurors, the 2 holdouts were NOT the people of color.

The judge wanted them to go back and keep trying to reach a verdict, so two days later they had finally convinced the last two holdouts to vote to acquit as well. They even had a chance to find the officer guilty of reckless discharge of a weapon endangering Castile's girlfriend and little girl. They still voted to acquit even though he shot 7 times, one of the bullets narrowly missing the little girl. How? Why? I would love to have a recording of those deliberations. Since I don't, I will let the legal system take care of it and hopefully there will be recourse that poor family can take. It just seems so unfair.

Now I will say this much. I was watching the news last night and they were showing that there was a huge protest march after the jury came back with its' verdict. Obviously, it did not go over well. For the most part, the march was peaceful. Yes, this is a good thing. I don't think violence ever accomplishes anything, so I was pleased. I understand that they blocked traffic on the I-94 so they had to be moved to a different location which they did, but only after 18 people were arrested, including two reporters who were apparently there photographing the entire march. They said that it appeared that the majority of the people in the march were white. That gave me hope. I think most people are kind and do not think like the loud mouths we hear from the most. Maybe the kind ones need to be louder. It's just a thought.

My point is this. I hate talking about this stuff. I really do. It hurts me. Why you ask? Because I see us going backwards instead of forward. We fought to get rid of racism. Oh sure, it's always been there, but at least people were more apt to keep their thoughts to themselves and they were civil. Not anymore. People say whatever they feel wherever they are. They make no apologies for it either.

Yes, we've started on this downhill slope for some time now; but oddly enough I believe it became most obvious when President Obama took office. Was it HIS fault? Not in the least. I'm just saying it's when we started to see racism become more visible and without regret.

I first started to notice it when he was first elected. Instead of just being happy that we just voted for a highly principled, intelligent, funny and honorable man as President of our country, we instead began to pat ourselves on the back for voting for a black man. It really made me angry in a way. Not enough to throw something, mind you; but enough to be annoyed. I thought we were more advanced than that. I thought we were at a place where we could look beyond the color of a person's skin and see them for who they are. Instead, we made it all about race.

Then of course, came the "birther" movement. That was 5 years of fun. It virtually gave people the freedom to say racially explicit things that we never would have normally said prior to that. Unless of course, you're talking about prior to the 70's. I know Trump makes an easy target, but let's face it; he led the charge on this one.

He made one false accusation after another. He kept claiming to have proof that our President was not a citizen and demanded time after time that our President produce his birth certificate. The President complied. After the first time, Trump then claimed it wasn't the "legal" form and demanded another one. Again, the President complied. Then Trump demanded to see his College Diploma. I mean, really? This is the first time in history that we have ever demanded such details from a sitting President. Are we to believe that it's just a coincidence that he is the first black President? Maybe it truly is, but it seems awfully odd to me. Now that Trump is President, isn't it strange how the tables have turned? He won't even show his tax returns. He doesn't think we want to see them. I DO!!

So, enough with the racism topic. As I said, this is a topic I feel very strongly about and I hate to sound so preachy, but I am passionate about certain topics. This is one of them. There was no way to make this chapter funny or even entertaining as the subject matter is just too heavy. I'll see what I can do with the next chapter. Fingers crossed!

CHAPTER 18

Separation of Church and State

Ok, fine. I decided to dive straight from racism into the hysterically funny topic of separation of church and state. I knew you'd get a charge out of this one. Well, hang on to your hats kids. You may even need one of those elastic things to go around your tummy to keep from getting a hernia from all your laughter. Fasten your seat belts, here we go!

First, has anyone other than myself noticed that there no longer seems to be a separation between church and state. There used to be. At some point, we seem to have lost it. I mean, we've really "lost it". All throughout the campaign we heard about abortion, birth control and Planned Parenthood and even babies being dismembered (which turned out to be a falsehood about Planned Parenthood, after all was said and done). Since when are these political issues? I think that these are some of the most personal issues a person should ever have to deal with and yet suddenly the government is all over them.

Mind you, this is the Republican Party. The same party that wants LESS regulation. Yet they sure seem to like to know what's going on in everyone's bedroom, don't they? It's the same with the LBGT community. Why is that? Shouldn't that be a religious or even a medical issue? Why does the government have to be involved? Just give them their human rights and leave them alone. It isn't up to the government to decide if they are sinners. Only God can do that. Planned Parenthood has provided many teenagers with advice and preventive measures to avoid teenage pregnancies. This has saved the states who knows how much money in Medicaid for unwanted babies that these young women could not afford to raise on their own.

Why would you pull funding for such a wonderful program? They are not an abortion clinic. They perform mammograms, pap smears and give advice to women who would otherwise not be able to afford it. They are life savers for the poor. Some of them do offer abortions, but at least they are done in a safe setting. I would not choose abortion as an alternative for myself, but I would never judge someone who did. I can't imagine how I would react if I had a 13-year-old daughter who had been raped and got pregnant. I think if she told me she didn't want it, I'd run her down to the clinic so fast it would make your head spin.

Another scenario would be if a young mother of 2 was pregnant with her third child and something went wrong during childbirth where the doctors could only save either the mom or the baby, but not both. I would hate to be the dad; but if I were, I would choose the mom. Why? Why would you choose to leave 2 little kids at home motherless? I don't believe that it's more important to save the life that has yet to take a breath outside the womb as opposed to the one who has already been living and breathing and formed relationships and is loved by so many people. How does that make any sense? That dad will then be alone raising 3 little kids all by himself, including one infant which he could possibly come to resent since he lost his wife because of the baby's birth. He will be grieving the loss of his wife and trying to raise his family all alone. What a nightmare. Yes, I understand abortion under certain conditions. Now you may ask, what religion am I? Good question. Can I plead the fifth?

I prefer to answer that question as simply stating that I am Christian. Christian covers many religions and I prefer not to pigeon hole myself into any particular one. That said, I was raised a very strict Catholic. I went to Catholic grade school and as a result, attended church every weekday and

Sunday. I also went to confession every Saturday. If a Holy Day happened to fall on a Saturday; well, I went to church on Saturday too. In other words, I attended mass 6 or 7 days a week.

When I was a child, my mother was not a Catholic. Back in the day, the Catholic Church believed that if you were not Catholic you were going to Hell. As such, I would go to school each day and be taught that my mom was going to go to Hell because she was not a Catholic. When I would come home from school, my dad would make me sit on my mom's lap and beg her to become a Catholic so she wouldn't go to Hell. It's very hard for me to try to explain how much of an impact this had on me being such a young child. This should never happen to such a small child, but back then it just seemed normal. My dad didn't know any better.

It left a mark on me that still lives with me to this day. My mother became a Catholic when I turned about 12 or 13. I remember my mom surprising my dad as he had no idea she'd been taking classes. He was so thrilled; almost as thrilled as my paternal grandparents. Of course, so was I. It meant she wasn't going to go to Hell anymore. Hallelujah!

My family was involved in a fatal car accident when I was 19. I was the oldest of 4 children. My mother was killed in that accident. Even now, my siblings and I carry the scars of that accident. Some physical and most emotional. I remember praying the rosary a lot after that accident. It gave me a considerable amount of comfort at that time. One evening shortly after I got out of the hospital my Dad said to me that he thought that God had "taken" mom early because he felt she may have been falling away from the Catholic Church. I believe that was the last time I picked up my rosary. The lessons I learned from Catholic school and Church and the lessons I learned from home were let's just say somewhat hypocritical. Yes, I am Christian. I am not however, Catholic. I have many reasons. Reasons I'm sure you're not interested in and since this isn't meant to be a lesson in religion; let's not go there.

I do not have any issue whatsoever with Churchgoers. I even admire them. I wish I got that same kind of comfort that they get. Instead, I just start to shake like a leaf. Something is obviously wrong, so I don't go. I still follow the 10 commandments and say my prayers and I live according to the way I believe God would want me to. I choose not to show my face at Church on Sunday and then go home and shout obscenities or pick a fight with someone. That's hypocritical. I think God would prefer my way rather than see me in Church just so I can say, "yes, I go to church". If you don't "live" your religion; don't bother going to church. At least, that's my theory.

No matter what, church is church and state is state. The two are separate and should remain that way. I do not want the government sticking their nose in where it doesn't belong.

The Republicans have fought tooth and nail to keep the government from interfering with their Second Amendment Rights (guns), but when it comes to Religion; bring it on. Why is that? Shouldn't all the Amendments be treated the same way? I'm no expert, but I'm pretty sure that was the intention when the Constitution was first written. Of course, I wasn't born yet, so there's always a chance I could be mistaken. From the looks of some of our Congressmen and women, I have a feeling that some of them may have been around when the document was signed. Can you say, "shorter terms"?

CHAPTER 19

Wall? What Wall?

I'm sure we all remember Candidate Trump talking about the big, beautiful wall he was going to build between the U.S. and Mexico, right? You know the one I'm referring to. Remember? The one that Mexico was going to pay for. That one.

What ever happened to that stupid thing anyway? Not that I really care, mind you. I don't happen to think walls work. After all, does anyone remember the Great Wall of China or the Great Berlin Wall? Those weren't exactly models of success. Or were they? Maybe it just depends on your perspective. Either way, somebody still has to pay for this monstrosity and the President of Mexico has made it very clear that it is NOT going to be Mexico. Gee, I don't know why the very people we are trying to keep out wouldn't want to pay the cost for the Big Beautiful Wall. They are so darned selfish!

So, after admitting that he hadn't discussed the payment of the wall with the Mexican President; Candidate Trump then came back to Arizona and boasted how Mexico is going to pay for that darned wall, "they just don't know it yet". They didn't know because he forgot to tell them. He's so silly sometimes. After weeks of this ridiculous nonsense, he finally admitted that the American taxpayers were going to have to pay for the wall first, but Mexico would reimburse us. When pressed as to when this was going to happen, since the Mexican President was still saying "no way", Trump finally came up with some lame story about how we would recover the money in some other way. This means that the government might recoup some small portion, but the people are NEVER going to see their tax dollars again. It's code. Sometimes I just crack myself up.

Personally, when, and if they do decide to build this thing, I really hope it isn't gold plated with Trump's name plastered all over it. I don't think I can handle it. Besides, what's the point in making this thing so beautiful anyway. Is it going to be any better at keeping anybody out if it's beautiful? No, of course not. What it will do is give the drug dealers something pretty to look at as they're moving their product through the tunnels running underneath the Big Beautiful Wall. I'm already afraid that he's going to rebuild all our airports and rename them all after himself. You know what I mean. Just imagine it. Trump International Airport NY, Trump International Airport Phoenix, Trump International Airport Dallas, etc., etc. I can close my eyes and see the big gold letters in my imagination. Can't you? He's like a dog leaving a mark everywhere he goes. I guess we should be grateful he doesn't pee on stuff and leave it at that. Ok, I'm done now.

Psych! Not done. Just thought of a great idea. What if we built a big wall around Washington? It wouldn't cost the taxpayers nearly as much and I'm guessing we'd probably be less at risk from the illegals crossing the Mexican border than we are from our own Congressmen and women right now. See? I can be smart when I want.

CHAPTER 20

Sean Spicer Revisited

I know I have addressed Sean Spicer in Chapter Four entitled "The Pres and the Press" but given what I heard on the news today, I felt we needed to revisit what is going on in the White House Briefing Room. I have been trying very hard not to make any comparisons of the Trump administration to the Nixon years, but this is now impossible. The Trump White House has now banned all cameras and audio from the briefing room. Today, Sean Spicer actually took a question from a Russian reporter and refused to take any questions from CNN. You may not like CNN, CBS, NBC, ABC, FOX or whatever other American network there may be, but the American taxpayers pay the salaries for the press secretary. Did you know that? I'll admit that I did not until tonight. They work for the people, not for the President. While they report whatever the President tells them to report, it is still the people of America they answer to. Who knew? In any case, the buck still stops with the President, as he is the one who dictates what gets reported and what does not and how.

I'm sure that many people think that it's perfectly understandable for the President not to want any video or audio of his press briefings because the press has been so mean to him. If you honestly believe that to be a valid excuse, you would have to believe that no President should have press briefings with video or audio. The press was not kind to President Clinton. Does anybody remember the famous blue dress? I thought so. The press was terrible to President Bush. Remember Iraq? Yep. As far as Obama is concerned; I don't think Fox News ever had a kind word to say about that man once. Yet he took questions from them at every briefing but one when he had to leave early. It wasn't just Fox either. The rest of the news stations were tough on him too.

The press doesn't go to these briefings with the intent to be "mean". They go into them with the tough questions that need to be answered. They are representatives of the "people". That's us. It is their job to get the hard answers. They aren't there to beat up on the press secretary or even the President. They are simply there to get answers to the tough questions, even if it sometimes makes the White

House uncomfortable. If the White House isn't doing anything wrong, they should not have anything to be so defensive about and they shouldn't be afraid to have their questions and answers recorded for replay at a later date.

The real reason President Trump doesn't want these press briefings shown or heard is because he has been caught in so many lies just by simply replaying tapes of his own words or press briefings that were given. He thinks that if the public can't hear or see these words; it will be his word against the "FAKE NEWS". Who's going to believe Fake News over the President, right? This is called a direct violation of the Constitution. The Freedom of the Press is being threatened and we should all be alarmed, whether we like Trump or not.

Not since the Nixon years have we seen the Press be so oppressed. This should alarm us all. DING DING DING!!!

On another note, it is rumored that Sean Spicer may be leaving the Press Secretary's podium to take on a different position within the West Wing. I have no idea if this will be a demotion, promotion, if he's leaving of his own will or if he's been asked to leave or if he's even leaving at all. My word! I think I might be happy for the guy. As I said previously, I think he's a heart attack waiting to happen. I hope whatever he ends up doing is less stressful. He seems like a nice enough guy, just in the wrong position. Let me explain why I say this.

As I understand it, if you are a journalist, chances are your dream job is to someday become the Press

Secretary for the White House. Sean Spicer had his dream come true. Unfortunately, he is working for a President who is now making him do things that he knows go squarely against everything he believes in regarding the Freedom of the Press. He has worked with many of the people in that briefing room that he now is being told he cannot take questions from. This is going against all his principles. Many of these very people are people he once called "friends". Can you imagine how this makes him feel? He must feel like a traitor on some level.

I heard from one of the reporters on CNN who was a friend of Sean's, that he is a great husband and dad and a nice man. If you have watched his briefings, every so often you will get a glimpse of his humor and see him smile or joke. I think that's the "real" Sean.

The Sean that cuts people off and snaps at people and refuses answers is the Sean that is trying to please his "boss". I am trying to cut him some slack. I think at some point in our careers we all wish we could have a "do-over". I know I do.

I do wish he would leave the White House altogether, but I don't see that happening, as I'm sure the money is just too good to pass up. Must be nice, huh? I wonder how much we're paying him. I just hope we don't get stuck paying Huckabee-Sanders, but I bet we do. Oh well, I don't plan on losing sleep over it. I lose sleep over other stuff.

This Page Intentionally Left Blank

CHAPTER 21

Hey Mikey – What did you do?

Anybody want to talk about Michael Flynn? I like to call him Little Mikey myself. I know, I know. That really isn't very respectful, is it? After all, the guy was a Lt. General. Shouldn't he be treated with a certain amount of respect? NOPE! Respect needs to be earned and even at his level, he has not earned it. From what I have learned of Flynn, he was a bit of a wild card if you will.

He did serve in the U.S. Army for 33 years, so for that I will give him credit. Unfortunately, he did not always serve his country well and there lies the rub (or so they say). In 2012, he was elected to the Defense Intelligence Agency. He submitted his retirement papers in 2014, although he was apparently forced out about a year before, as he was known to be abusive to his staff, worked against policy, didn't listen and had bad management skills.

When President Trump and President Obama had spoken, President Obama advised Trump not to place Flynn in a position that would allow him access to sensitive information. Trump decided to do the opposite. As you can see, it worked well. He loves the guy. Why? Well, that's a very good question. I can't figure it out for the life of me.

It appears that President Obama may have had Little Mikey all wrong, however. I think he might just be the perfect guy to put in a position for top secret material. After all, this guy is awesome at keeping secrets! Well, at least he's very good at keeping them FROM the government. Whether he'd be good at keeping them FOR the government could be something entirely different.

It seems that Mr. Flynn failed to mention a few things on a very important form he filled out when being considered for the position as National Security Advisor. Nothing major, mind you. Just small stuff like involvement with foreign dignitaries abroad in Russia, Turkey and now even the Middle East. Apparently, he's in a whole lot of hot water, that wild and crazy guy.

You may (or may not) recall at the beginning of my book that I stated I had a bad feeling about Flynn from the first time Trump named him as his National Security Advisor. There was just something "off" about him. He reminded me of a teenage boy on uppers or something. He was out of control. I tend to trust my gut, but always leave room to change my mind.

In Flynn's case, my mind never wavered. So far at least, it seems my instincts were correct. Oops! I hate it when people say I told you so. I really didn't mean it to sound that way, but sheesh! This guy is just so darned easy to read. I don't even read that well and I could read him! Maybe he has ADHD or something.

According to the news, rumor has it that Flynn is currently cooperating with the FBI regarding the Russia investigation. I'd love to be a fly on the wall during that questioning, wouldn't you? Of course, as I've stated before, just because he's under oath doesn't mean he's incapable of telling a lie. After all, it's only perjury if he gets caught. Right? I think that's how it goes.

I just hope this whole situation gets sorted out soon so our Government can get back to work instead of spending all our taxpayer time and money on all of these investigations. Yes, I want to know what, if anything, illegal happened. If it did, those responsible need to be held accountable. Let's just move it along already. How long does this have to take? How many years must we wait for this? We already know the players. Quit messing around with the open hearings and just bring them in front of

Mueller so we can get the answers to the hard questions. Yeah, yeah, yeah. I know. Everybody wants to watch the hearings. Fine. I'll behave now. I just can't promise for how long. It never lasts.

CHAPTER 22

Wanna Play a Game?

It seems our President just loves to joke around. He has a wonderful sense of humor apparently. He gets the biggest charge out of playing games with the press and even the people of this country. He teases us consistently with little innuendos. I will give you his latest. He "hinted" that there were tapes or recordings of Comey in the White House during their conversation when Trump supposedly asked Comey to "let it go" when referring to the Flynn investigation.

According to Comey, he was then asked by Trump for his loyalty. Of course, Trump denies that he ever did this and has basically accused Comey of perjury since Comey testified to this under oath. Comey has been described as being as honest as they come and very trustworthy. Since Trump lies with practically every breath he takes, my bet is that Comey is telling the truth here. We won't know of course until all the hearings are completed and even then, we may still not know the entire truth, right? After all, it's just a matter of who you decide to believe isn't it?

Once Comey heard of this tweet by the President, it prompted him to leak his written memos to the press so he could get his story out ahead of any tapes in order to clarify any misunderstandings. His hope was to prompt an investigation by a special counsel, which it did. Over the past few weeks, Trump has been asked over and over if these tapes truly exist. Each time he is very coy and skirts the issue extremely carefully by saying things like "I'll be letting you know very soon and you'll be very, very disappointed" or something to that effect. Really? Why didn't he just say "no, I don't have any tapes myself; but that doesn't mean that the other intelligence agencies didn't record us". That, I would not have any knowledge of. Instead, he just makes a big game out of it.

I swear he just enjoys dangling these things over the peoples' heads, just like you would hold a piece of cheese over a dog's head. I swear, someday somebody is going to bite his tiny little fingers. I warned you I couldn't be nice for too long, didn't I? At least I'm honest. I may not be nice, but I'm honest. That must count for something. Yes? No? Oh well.

Either way, I don't like these games he plays. Sure, you could make the claim that he feels vindicated because the press isn't "nice to him". What he doesn't seem to realize is that he isn't just messing with the press. He's messing around with the entire country. This includes his base.

Sure, I'm certain they aren't as upset as the rest of us are, but I'm almost positive that if you were to ask them, most would have answered that they wish he would have just answered honestly to begin with rather than hint around. Of course, I'm just as positive that a good many of them will also say "who cares?". That seems to be a fairly standard answer among many Trump supporters. This is something that deeply disturbs me. We should all care. You can like him and still care. It's possible. Give it a shot!

For me? I'd rather be out playing tag in the front yard. Too bad I'm too darned old to run anymore. Everything hurts now. So instead I sit and annoy people. This, I love.

Did that sound like the end of the chapter by any chance? Fooled ya! As a matter of fact, it was supposed to be exactly that. It would seem that darned news just keeps changing as I go along and I have to keep adding stuff. So, I'm afraid we're still stuck on the same chapter for just a little bit longer. Bear with me, ok?

According to the news (no, not just CNN) and I mean all the news stations, we now have irrefutable truth that it was in fact Putin who ordered the hack of the DNC with the sole intention of influencing our election in favor of Donald Trump. This is not to say that his attempt was successful or that Trump did not win honestly; it is merely to say that the intent was there. Trump won the election by winning the electoral colleges votes pure and simple and nobody can take that away from him, no matter how badly they may want to or how unfair they may feel this election was tainted.

The fact is, even a re-election would probably not change the outcome. You may think I'm a little off my preverbal rocker for saying that, but it's what I believe. Why? Too many people were already a little "iffy" when it came to vote for Hillary. Once the emails and other false stories broke, due in part to Russia's involvement, these feelings were just strengthened. Those thoughts are still there in many people's heads, true or not, and a lot of people still think those stories were not lies. She is still seen as a liar in many people's eyes. It boggles my mind considering how much more Trump lies, but I think it's true. I just don't get it, that's all.

The other thing I don't get is our President's nonchalant attitude toward this intrusion by the Russian government. Is he so afraid that this is going to make his Presidency look illegitimate that he would rather let a foreign government hack our government's servers rather than address the problem? That's just whacky! Why exactly is our President just so fond of Putin? At first, he seemed to want to be best buds with the guy.

His opinion of Putin seems to have cooled to some degree, but he is still very hesitant to confront him on a military level, even after finding out that Russia has been aiding the Assad Regime in Syria. He just seems to give Putin break after break. My best guess is that we need to follow the money people. But what do I know. If you followed MY money, you wouldn't even make it to the corner gas station. Let's see if I can end this chapter this time. Onward and Upward!

CHAPTER 23

Collusion/Corruption/ Obstruction

This White House has sure been filled with a lot of well, let's just say suspicious activity. So many of the President's Men are being currently investigated for some type of Russian Collusion, Obstruction of Justice or just plain old Corruption.

Oh sure, I love to watch the public hearings. They're all so interesting, minus of course the boring parts where the Senators get all long-winded. I don't like that part so much. I also don't care for it when they refuse to let a person finish a sentence to answer a question just because they may not like the answer. That goes for both sides I might add. It's the little things, you know what I mean?

Basically, I find them very informative. That said however, I still believe that most of these hearings should be held in a closed setting with Mueller at the helm. I realize that the American people have a right to know a lot of the information revealed; but we do NOT have the right to the classified information.

Besides, it seems to me that when a sitting President is speaking in private to one of his staff, he should have an expectation to a certain amount of privacy. Now, when an investigation is underway for criminal activity, all bets are off obviously. That still doesn't mean that the people need to hear these conversations. These conversations should still be protected under a closed hearing. At least that makes more sense to me. The way things are being done now with some public and others closed; it seems that we are just having two hearings instead of just one to prevent any classified information from being revealed to the public. Won't this just take twice as long? What's the point? If Mueller holds the hearings, he can decide which information is safe to share with the public and we will still get our curiosity satisfied, just not as quickly. Patience people, Patience!

Most recently, we found out that indeed our President is being investigated for possible obstruction of justice. Of course, he believes this is all another "witch hunt". He loves that word almost as much as he loves the word "fake news". Nixon also used the word "witch hunt" a lot and of course we all know how that ended. This is not to suggest that the same thing is sure to happen to Trump, but you know that old saying, "if it walks like a duck and quacks like duck", well.....need I say more? There is just a little too much hinky stuff going on in this White House for my comfort level. I'm not trying to jump to any false conclusions, but my gut is telling me that something smells rotten here.

The reason I have such a bad feeling about this White House is quite simple. There is just too much secrecy. Oh sure, I keep hearing that he is the most accessible of any President. Is he? His only real communication with the average American is through Twitter. His only other communications have come through his rallies to his base only. You never hear him speak to a crowd with anyone who doesn't have the same mindset. If a dissenter somehow manages to sneak into one of his rallies, they are immediately removed by security. Is this what you call transparency? I sure don't. I think this President can't handle the heat. He is only willing to listen to people who are followers/loyalists. Don't even dare to disagree. If you do, you will be called a name or mocked. That is his M.O.

Why do the American people put up with it? Well, I do not have a clue. His supporters think he's funny or they simply don't care. Why that is, I have no idea. They SHOULD care. We should all care how the leader of the greatest country in the world conducts himself, but they don't for whatever reason. Some say he's "refreshing" because he says what the average American is thinking. I'm not so sure I agree with that statement. He may be speaking for some, but certainly not for the majority. I'm about as average as they come and he sure as heck doesn't speak for me, that's for darned sure.

We've all made mistakes in our lives when we say things we wish we could take back. God knows I sure have. I've lost two of my best friends over something stupid I did or said because of my twisted sense of humor. If I could take it back, I would do it in a heartbeat. Sadly, once the words come out of your mouth, you can't put them back in. Oh, I apologized alright. I spent years beating myself up over it until I finally had to realize that I had made a terrible mistake and I just had to learn from it and forgive myself just like I would if someone had wronged me. It took me a while to get there, but I did it. (Well almost)

I don't see any qualities in Trump that show him capable of regret. Instead, he just continues to place blame on others or tell more lies to try to make excuses for himself.

Once we found out that it was certain that Putin was indeed responsible for the hacking of the DNC, instead of immediately acknowledging Russia's responsibility and coming up with a plan for sanctions or other forms of punishment; Trump jumped at another chance to blame Obama. Again, with the blame game.

I don't know about you, but I am sick of the blame game from both sides of the aisle, but mostly from the President himself. He is Commander-in-

Chief of our country and as such, should be taking responsibility most of the time, but this guy NEVER takes responsibility. What the heck is wrong here? I will agree that I wish Obama had taken a stronger stance once he learned of Russia's influence over the election. Do I understand that he was afraid it would look like he was trying to influence the election? Sure, I do. I'm sure he wishes he had acted too.

Hindsight is always better than foresight, right? According to the news, he and his team had to struggle with the decision as the information could spark Russia to do even more damage. I'm not sure if that makes sense to me, but I'm sure it does if you know more about the military and government. I still think it comes down more to not wanting to be seen as doing anything to influence the election. Besides, what did he have to lose? At that point, Hillary was still in the lead and no machines were tampered with, right? WRONG! WRONG! WRONG! The jokes on us. Never count your chickens until the eggs are hatched, right? OY!

So, let's just say that it's all Obama's fault that the election was tampered with like Trump says. Does this mean that Trump should just sit back and let it all go now and pretend that nothing happened since his "election" wasn't hampered and he is in fact, a legitimate President? No, of course it doesn't. At least it doesn't to anybody with any common sense. Russia has been doing this not just to the United States, but to France and Britain as well. Who knows how many other countries? I can't keep up with them. Whenever Kellyanne or Spicer are asked what the President is doing, we always get some idiotic answer along the lines of "well, there was no collusion" or "I haven't had that conversation with the President yet".

Are they for real? CNN did report that in fact, the President did sign an executive order to require some sort of Cyber Protection. I think I have that right, but I could be wrong because my brain can only hold so much at one time. Now, why don't they just say that? It would sure make the President look a whole lot better, wouldn't it? They sure aren't doing him any favors by arguing with the press all the time. It just makes him look even worse than he really is. At least that's my two cents worth. I'd give you a dime, but times are tough!

As far as the rest of the President's men are concerned, we will just have to wait and see how it all shakes out after the hearings are over. I'm trying not to jump to any conclusions, but if I'm being honest, I think I may have already taken the leap. Like I said before, follow the money trail and I think we will find our answers there.

We have voted a man into office that has many business ties to some of the countries that I previously referred to as "frienemies". I believe that's why there is so much secrecy and why these conflicts of interest exist. I think his business interests are influencing some of his political decisions and the country be damned. Sometimes I can be very smart. Of course, this may not be one of those times. We'll just have to wait and see.

One thing is for certain, his Cabinet is very loyal to him. I will say that. I do believe that if push comes to shove however, Mattis and McManus will eventually come forward if at any point they feel Trump is putting this country at risk. The point is, how long will it take before they fully realize the extent of his actions?

If we know anything, Trump is very tight-lipped when it comes to certain information. He knows who he can trust within his inner-circle and with what information. Kushner knows more than any of them, mark my word. My word isn't worth much, but you can still mark it if you'd like. Ok, I'm done now. Next!

CHAPTER 24
MY View of THE View

Unlike most people, I have never truly figured out exactly what it is that I want to be when I grow up. I guess it's a little late now, huh? I was always terrible at literature, but very good at grammar. Now wouldn't you think if you were good at one you'd be good at the other? I guess not. My comprehensive skills were always lacking, but I did love to write. I wish someone had told me that there was actually a career to be had in journalism. The thought just never occurred to me.

Now that I'm 68, I finally figured out what I want to be. Too late? I guess we'll see. Hopefully not.

Whenever someone would talk about their dream jobs, for the longest time I literally had nothing to say. Finally, it dawned on me. I absolutely love watching the ladies of "The View". Oh sure, they all talk at once and sometimes it's hard to distinguish who said what; but I still love it. Do I always agree with them? Don't be silly. Of course not.

My favorite is Joy Behar. I don't always agree with her either, but even when I disagree, I think she's funny as all get out. It makes it easier to swallow. Of course, who doesn't like Whoopi? She's a hoot. Sunny is the smart one. I sometimes think she's a little snobbish, but she's no doubt smart as heck. Jed took a long time for me to get used to, but now I like her. I often find myself defending her out loud in my own living room (yes, I'm a little crazy like that) when the others gang up on her. Even if I don't agree with her, I still think she makes some valid points and at the very least deserves to be heard. Once I hear her out, then I tell her she's wrong. Again, I'm a little nutty.

We can't forget Sarah as she is also one of my favorites. She is just so darned sweet and always seems to be so level headed. She always tries to remain the "calm among the storm" if you will. She'd make a great negotiator. She always manages to find some middle ground that all can agree on. I like that. I wish Congress could work that way.

Paula is sweet too even though I rarely agree with her political views. She's pretty low key and doesn't get too riled up over things. She's not on too often anymore, so we don't really see too much of her, but I like her as well. Like I said, I just love watching the show. The "Hot Topics" are my favorite.

So, one day some friends were talking about their dream jobs and it finally occurred to me that I would just love to be on a panel of a talk show. Of course, they all looked at me like I was from outer space because it's not exactly something you'd expect to hear from someone who has been raised in the Midwest most of her life and spent the majority of her career doing clerical work. I mean, seriously? Who do I think I am anyway? A movie star? Let's get real!

If people don't want an answer, maybe they shouldn't ask. Right? After all, I'm not asking to be the host. I just want to be part of the panel. I suppose I could be the host. God knows I have a big enough mouth for it; but no! I just want to be part of the panel. Is that asking for too much? I think it just may be. After all, who wants to listen to an opinionated 68-year-old unknown spout off? I probably wouldn't. I can be pretty funny sometimes though. It just depends on your sense of humor. It's definitely not for everyone. I have what they call a dry sense of humor. That's basically code for saying a lot of people don't think I'm funny. I'll say something funny with a completely straight face. Most people know right away from my tone of voice that it's a joke. Others, not too sure. It may take them a while. Some would say my humor is an acquired taste. I acquired it at about the age of 10.

I also enjoy watching "The Talk", but since politics is more up my alley, I definitely lean more toward "The View". I would love to just be a guest someday on that show. Maybe if my book makes any headway, I'll get my chance. Fingers crossed! (and no, my thumbs are not up).

CHAPTER 25

Healthcare or Lack of?

Well, the Senate has finally made the big reveal of the new and improved Healthcare Act passed by the House. I still haven't quite gotten all the details to be perfectly honest; but I sure have heard a lot of commotion. It's not exactly going down like a bowl of ice cream, let's just put it that way.

The mandate is gone. That could be a good thing, but it also means that premiums will go up. Many of the healthcare "essentials" are still being left to the states. This will also raise premiums. They did however, continue to cover pre-existing and cover children living at home up to age 26. That's good. For reasons I fail to understand, the largest tax credits are going to a small portion of the very richest people in the country. Somebody is really going to have to come up with a good explanation for that one. No more subsidies, but people within a certain tax bracket will get tax credits at the end of year. Sadly, this will not help them the first year when they must fork out those higher premiums and deductibles. They may get some of it back at the end of the year, but how do they pay for it in the meantime?

The whole idea I guess is to create competition. I remember how well that worked when we deregulated the banks too. It was supposed to force the banks to charge LESS interest and fees to stay competitive. Eventually, the big banks ate up all the little banks and everybody just started raising their interest rates and fees through the roof. Why? Because nobody had any control over them anymore and they could charge anything they wanted. There was a time when banks were only charging an average of about 7% on charge cards. Slowly but surely, those rates raised to anywhere from 12% to 14% on average. This is good old competition I suppose. Let's see who can charge the most and make the most money the fastest!

The last I heard, there were still five Republicans were not willing to sign this new and improved bill. Three of them would need to change their minds before it will pass. I will be perfectly honest here. I haven't gone to the website to see exactly what is and isn't covered; so, I am in no position to make any judgement here. I only know bits and pieces of it. My reason? Simply put, it doesn't apply to me at this time of my life. I have never been so thrilled to be OLD!! Thank goodness for Medicare. That's all I can say. I do know that Medicare was not well-received when it was first rolled out, so I can certainly understand why a bill of this size is going to take more time to perfect. Even Medicare isn't perfect and it's been around for a long time. Our only hope is that our Congress will somehow see the light and start to play nice with one another. Yes, I know. A girl can dream, can't she?

I will admit that I wish that Congress had not made this a political issue, but more of a humanitarian issue. This is our health and welfare we are talking about. Ever since Trump started to campaign, he has done nothing but talk about "repealing and replacing" Obamacare. Why couldn't he just have said "The Affordable Care Act" is not working. We need to fix it and go from there. That's something we all could have agreed on. I don't think you'll find one Democrat that will tell you that Obamacare/ACA was perfect. We all agreed that the original bill required a lot of work. Let's be honest however, the bill was NOT a complete and total failure.

Obamacare saved a lot of people that would never have been able to otherwise obtain insurance coverage due to either pre-existing conditions or premiums that were simply too high. The groundwork was already laid. Trump kept saying he had something so much better and it was going to be "so easy". Another lie. He didn't have ANYTHING. He later said, "who knew it would be so hard". Well, just about everybody but him apparently. To

Trump, it was all about getting rid of anything that had Obama's name on it, once again. So, we just threw away the baby with the bathwater instead of just giving the baby a bath. That's just DUMB! He could have had the support of the Democrats if only he had approached it differently. Politics is just stupid sometimes. Both sides need a time-out!

CHAPTER 26

And it's a Wrap!

Well, as much fun as this has been, I'm afraid I might be getting dangerously close to either annoying the crap out of you or simply boring you to death. So, I think it time to wrap this puppy up and say "good-bye".

Before I do, I would like to say a few words regarding my own personal perspective. While it's highly unlikely, I hope that at least one member of Congress reads this book even if it's just to read a few chapters, particularly this one.

I have lived a rather normal middle class to lower middle class most of my life. I have been blessed in more ways than I can count, but never monetarily. At best, I was comfortable.

I have always lived pretty much from paycheck to paycheck and sometimes those checks didn't make it to the end of the month. Was that the government's fault? No. Was it my fault? To some degree, but it was also due to one heck of a lot of misfortune and things I had no control over. I believe that I have had a life that is far better than most, but far worse than others. I am middle class.

The only thing that makes me feel better right now is knowing that I am now in the same tax bracket as Trump. He doesn't have to pay taxes and neither do I. Gotcha! He apparently makes too much and I make too little. It must stink being rich, huh?

Maybe you've started to see where I'm going with this. I do not believe for one minute that the rich owe it to the rest of the country to take care of everyone else so they can sit back and relax. I worked most of my life until I made the decision to take an early retirement at age 62 due to illness.

My hope was it would be temporary and I would be able to return to work soon, even if it was a part-time job. Instead, I became more ill as time went by and eventually required surgery 5 years later after becoming so weak I could barely stand. Thankfully, I am now feeling much better, but still a little unsteady on my feet. I'll take that any day over what I was before. My point is this, at 68 getting a job is going to be a challenge given my current health. I am living on a lesser social security check because I had to take it out early. There are many people just like me all over this country. We didn't choose this life. I can't qualify for Medicaid because my income is something like $60 over the poverty level.

That's correct. I'm one of the wealthier ones apparently. You must make under $1000 monthly to qualify for Medicaid. I wonder how many people know that. There seems to be a misconception that it's easy as pie to get Medicaid/food stamps. No, it's not. You must be dirt poor. Sure, there are people on it that do not belong, of that, I am sure. They probably qualified when they first applied and when their status changed, never bothered to notify the government because quite frankly, they are still living in dire conditions. Is it right? Nope, not in the least. That happens to be fraud, folks. I do not condone fraud. That's an abuse of taxpayer money.

But the government does have a responsibility to people who fall through the cracks. There are many, many people just like myself that just make a little too much to get any assistance and yet still can't afford to live a decent life. Sometimes, their best recourse is to not try to help themselves at all just to get whatever little aid is available because it's worth more than they can make by working. How twisted is that?

So, the next time you see someone in the grocery store line using a card for government food stamps; do not judge. Remember that old adage, "until you've walked in another man's shoes". As for what the government can do, here's a real tongue twister. They have benefits through Medicare called Extra Help. There are 3 types. Briefly stated, this benefit helps people of lower incomes with their Medicare premiums, coinsurance and lower prescription costs, depending on which plan you qualify for.

Here's the kicker. You're allowed to own a home, but you can't have more than $8,000.00 in an IRA, 401K or savings. So, let's say someone owns a car that may be 10 years old and nothing more than a few pieces of furniture and the clothes on their back. Let's then say they had $20,000 in an IRA to last them for the rest of their life. If they were my age, that would sure go fast and they would be denied. Yet, somebody else could own a $300,000 home and have $7,000 in an IRA and they'd get approved. Does that make sense to you? These are laws that could be and should be corrected. Now if I'm correct, these numbers may change from state to state, so you might have to check with Medicare. Either way, this is messed up.

This of course, could all be going away completely now with the new Healthcare Act, since they are cutting Medicaid by $800 billion over the next several years. We'll just have to see what happens. Tom Price said that he believes that giving tax breaks to the wealthy is better for the economy than helping the poor. Since he's wealthy, I'm sure he does. My blood boils every time I see that man. If you truly want to cut the deficit, please don't do it by cutting off benefits to those of us who need the money the most. Try making the people who have the most money to begin with pay their fair share, instead of constantly giving them tax cuts. This just boggles my mind. In fact, I simply do not understand anyone who truly believes that this idea works for anyone other than the rich. If Robin Hood was alive, I'd vote for him for President. Why not? At least he ADMITTED he was a thief! That's more than our politicians are willing to admit.

My final message is a simple one. Congress needs to put the needs of the people ahead of the party. The party is not paying their salary and the party did not put them in office. "We the People of the United States of America" voted them into office, not the party. This goes for Republicans and Democrats alike. We are tired. We are tired of the gridlock. We are tired of the finger pointing and the games. We no longer care who is at fault. Just get your acts together and get back to doing the jobs you were elected to do.

We cannot get a straight answer out of any of you anymore. All we get is "well, Obama was way worse"; or "well, we've tried, but the Republicans won't let us in". Knock it off! We aren't stupid. (ok, maybe a couple of us are) Seriously though; I mean it has come to the point where people off the street are now running for office just because we are so darned fed up with our typical Washington politicians.

No more. We must have shorter Congressional terms. Our Congressmen and women have become far too complacent. They are so comfortable in their positions, they have no worries about being kicked out. It's high time we changed it. I hope Trump will keep his promise and do something to shorten Congressional terms. He can use his executive authority. Let's see if he does it. He'd score some big points for that one. Could someone please give me a hand off my soapbox now? Thanks!

ABOUT THE AUTHOR

This is the part that everybody usually skips, so I'm just going to have a little fun here, if you don't mind.

As I stated earlier, I was raised in the Midwest; Kenosha, Wisconsin to be exact. Many of my family members whom I adore, still reside there. My sister, brothers and myself never would have survived that horrible accident had it not been for the support of such a large and wonderfully supportive family. It is in large part a testament to them that I am here to write this crazy book at all. I was not born in Kenosha however.

I was born in Marian, Indiana. My parents moved from Marian to Columbus, Ohio when I was only three months old. I like to say that it's because I didn't like it there, but I'm not sure if that's actually the case. I think my dad's job may have played a larger role. Still, I'm sticking to my story. I like it better. I like to think I was an influential baby. Not to brag, but my baby pictures were darned cute.

If you're wondering where I got my slightly twisted sense of humor, let's just say my birth was somewhat unusual. I'm gonna blame the stupid doctor who decided to let me overcook a full month and nearly kill my mom. It's quite amazing that my poor mother had any affection for me at all when you consider my birth nearly killed her. She suffered from pre-eclampsia and apparently her legs had swollen to the size of watermelons, but her doctor still refused to start her early or do a C-Section. Back then, those procedures just weren't done as often or as easily as they are now; so instead, she had to wait a whole month past her due date until I finally decided it was time to get my little butt in gear. I've always been a little slow and generally if I'm 5 minutes late, you can consider me "on time".

From what I was told, my mother went into convulsions and nearly died. Several days later, they had to take us both home by ambulance. Since there were no ambulances available, guess how we got home? Oh, come on now! Try using your wildest imagination. I'll bet nobody guessed. Did anybody guess a hearse all decked out in pink? If so, ding, ding, ding! You're the proud winner of an 8lb 4oz baby girl! I told you I was overcooked. Stinks for you that baby is now a wrinkly 68-year-old. Look at the bright side, at least I'm not huge anymore.

We then moved to Louisville, Kentucky where life for me was to be forever changed. That's right. My parents had the nerve to try replacing me with another kid. My sister Phyllis and I fought like cats and dogs until we turned about 38. (just kidding) Seriously though, until we both moved out of our dad's home and married, I don't think we truly realized just how precious a sister truly is. Boy, I sure do now. I simply can't imagine my life without her. I love her selflessness and her generosity and most of all, her simple kindness. She is one of a kind.

Not too much after that, my parents decided to move again and again and voila', again another frickin' kid! This one was of course, a boy kid. I liked him better because I didn't have to share a room with this kid. So much better. Plus, Keith didn't try to boss me around all the time because for some reason, he seemed to understand his role. This is something my sister failed to do, even though she was three years younger. Go figure! She still does it, but now I just listen. It makes it so much easier. In writing this however, I just noticed that there seems to have been a pattern here. Every time my parents moved, another kid popped out. Hmmm. They must have really loved moving. I digress. My brother Keith and I are still very close and he too is a wonderful person in my life that I could never live without. We've always been that way.

My mom used to take us all for walks. The two youngest always cheated. They got to ride while I had to walk. The first thing you need to know is that both my sister and my brother had red hair. Not the real bright red hair, the kind of red hair that's just very pretty. Of course, you don't see a lot of natural redheads that often, so every time we took a walk people would stop to look at the cute "red-headed twins" in the stroller. As I stood there with my plain old brown hair and brown eyes and everybody googled and awed over my brother and sister, eventually someone would generally see the "pathetic looking" one and throw me a little bone like, "well, you're pretty too" or even worse "aren't you lucky to have such cute little siblings?" Were they for real? I wanted to push the stupid stroller over, but mom wouldn't take her eye off the cute little "redheads". Eeesh!

Another few years go by and again another baby. This one's kinda little though. I think there's something wrong with it. It's all red for one thing.

Are all babies like this? Of course, once he started to grow a little, the kid was pretty darned cute. Tiny, but really cute. They named it Billy. It didn't look like a Billy, but I went along with it anyway. Who was I to argue? I was only 8. I felt rather protective of it for some reason. Maybe because I thought my brother was too rough on him and my sister was, well, she was the bossy one, remember?

I am so thankful to have been blessed with the brothers and sister that I have. I love them all so very much and I have never doubted their love for me. Sure, we have our disagreements just like any other family, but they never last long and we always end up in a better place afterwards. Our love has never wavered and I don't ever see that happening.

Have I bored you yet? Just hang on a little longer, ok? I promise to try to keep things as entertaining as I can.

I married young at the age of 21 mainly because I needed to escape my home environment. No, nothing drastic. I was just miserable living in the same home where my mother had lived before she died. My dad did his level best, but he just wasn't equipped to be both mom and dad. I was only 19 at the time of the accident and God knows I sure wasn't ready to take on that responsibility. I wasn't a mature 19, not by a long shot.

When I first met my soon to be first husband about a year after the accident; he was my ticket out. I will admit that I had my doubts, but I really thought he loved me so I figured I might as well take the leap. After all, I had very low self-esteem and truly didn't think I'd ever find anyone else. I will not say I have any regrets since the marriage lasted nearly 19 years and we produced three absolutely wonderful children. My kids are by far my biggest and best accomplishment to date. Unfortunately, I can't really take much credit for them as I feel they just happened to turn out "in spite of me" rather than "because of me". I tell people I taught them by bad example. They watched me do everything wrong so they'd learn NOT to do that! See? Pretty clever, huh? I thought so.

I will not list their names as all of them have some crazy security issues. Like I said. They learned from their mother's bad habits, not my good ones. I do have a couple. My kids are all very nice looking too. This too, I cannot take credit for. The only ones in the family that ever looked even remotely like me were the dogs, as I have brown hair and eyes. You would think that would be dominant. NOPE! Not in my house. Blond and blue overrule brown and brown. What the heck? Sometimes a girl just cannot catch a break. That's ok. I've always loved my dogs. In fact, I remember quite a few days when I probably would have traded in a kid before the dog (especially that middle one).

When my husband divorced me at the ripe age of almost 40; I thought I would never recover. I wasn't a good role model for my kids to be honest. No, I didn't do anything terrible; but I did fall apart. I wish I'd been stronger for them. Instead, they had to be strong for me. My daughter, in particular. I put my children in an impossible position. For that, I still kick myself. I'm much better at forgiving others than myself. It's just the way it is. I'm still working on that. I guess you could say "I'm a work in progress".

I give my children all the credit in the world for having turned out as well as they did. My oldest was only 16 and my youngest 11 at the time. It was a terrible time for us all. Eventually, I managed to mend fences with my ex and we became friendly again. I'm so glad we had a chance to get to that point.

After a mere seven years, I finally met someone I thought would make my dreams come true. He seemed the exact opposite of my ex and in many ways, he really was. Sadly, that marriage came to an end as well after about 11 years. I've come to realize that I'm just not cut out for it. I do so much better with the four-legged variety. I just wish they lived longer.

This seems like it might be a good place to say "goodbye". Yes, let's do that. I've truly enjoyed writing this book. As this is my first attempt at book writing, I have no idea where this will lead me, but even if it doesn't get me anywhere; I can honestly say I had a good time writing it. It's about darned time I finally found a hobby! Thanks for reading my first book. I truly hope you enjoyed reading it at least half as much as I've enjoyed writing it. Let's hope there's a second. Finger's crossed.